MORE PRAISE FOR *The Road to Guadalupe*

"A poignant, electric, dusty kaleidoscope of holy saints, eccentric sinners, plastic flowers, votive candles, and miracles, all seen through the combined sensibilities of a nineteenth-century classical poet and a street-wise hustler. I did not want it to end."

—NANCY STEINBECK, author of
*The Other Side of Eden: Life with John Steinbeck*

"Eryk Hanut creates a delicious, delightful dance through the heart of the Mexican soul. Rich in imagery and detail, filled with intriguing characters who explode off the page, this book is an offering to Our Lady of Guadalupe. It appears that the pregnant goddess has given birth to a writer, immaculately and brilliantly."

—GABRIELLE ROTH, author of *Sweat Your Prayers*

"*The Road to Guadalupe* is a lovely book, thoroughly engaging, a personal and captivating traveler's tale. . . . In his vivid narrative, unafraid of ideas, Eryk Hanut finds his stay in Mexico City both an exploration of inquiry about the history and mystique of Our Lady of Guadalupe, Mother of God, Goddess of the Americas, and a search for a secure foundation for his own ever-vacillating faith. . . . Wonderful and memorable."

—LELIA LUCE

"This is by far the best book on Guadalupe I have ever read—totally unlike the others. A travelogue sparkling with Mexico's wild sensuality and eeriness, kind people, great pyramids, singers, and recipes. A story superbly written, in the tradition of great French novelists like Bernanos."

—MARY FORD-GRABOWSKY,
author of *Prayers for All People*

"Where I live, in the desert Southwest, the Virgin of Guadalupe is the most revered religious figure of all. When locals printed a bumper sticker proclaiming 'In Guad We Trust,' they weren't kidding. Eyrk Hanut's splendid account sheds light on the transformative, uplifting power behind the legend."

—LARRY DOSSEY, M.D., author of
*Healing Beyond the Body* and *Healing Words*

"A fascinating and sharply etched tale of a pilgrimage through both modern and sixteenth-century Mexico. . . . Hanut brings his shrewd eye for character, deft wit, and an outsider's gift for observation as he discovers Aztec history, religious mysticism, and folk witchcraft, all derived from the miraculous appearances of the Virgin of Guadalupe."

—JEANNETTE WATSON, editor of *Bookstore: The Life and Times of Jeannette Watson and Books & Co.*

"A profoundly sublime, vivid, and almost surreal tapestry of diverse strands. This is a journey for all committed voyagers of the heart, and reminds us that the Divine Feminine manifests unceasingly even in the midst of modern chaos."

—DOROTHY WALTERS, author of *Marrow of Flame* and *Unmasking the Rose: A Kundalini Initiation*

"There is a saying, amongst we Mexican-Americanas, that no longer will we agree to be Malinche; that is, to act like the young Nahua-Aztec woman enslaved by the conquistador Cortez and forced to be his translator in order to keep herself and her family alive; that we will no longer act the role of 'the conquered'; that it is time to get up off our knees and to walk upright in honor and pride. We believe that this reversal of hundreds of years of domination begins by truthtelling, by saying aloud and validating one's own insights, experiences and *historias,* as we see them, not as we have been pressured to see them.

"This is not only an eye-witness account, but a heart-witness account of the modern-day fools, crazies, usurpers, politicos, and holy people swirling around one of the most revered shrines in the world, that of La nuestra Señora, Our Lady of Guadalupe. Through his rich descriptions and insights into the smoke and mirrors, fiestas and dolors surrounding La Diosa of the Americas, Hanut also weaves in his own unfolding devotion to La Morenita, the Blessed Mother. The pictures he draws for us with his words are exceptionally smart, funny, often iconoclastic and loving at the same time. Layer by layer, he peels away the decades of overlay surrounding Her apparitions and brings forth again Her underlying meanings for those who often approach Her on their knees out of respect, but who often also return home, far taller and with hearts lifted higher than they have ever been before."

—CLARISSA PINKOLA ESTÉS, author of *Women Who Run with the Wolves*; and director, Sociedad de Nuestra Señora de Guadalupe

# THE ROAD TO GUADALUPE

*Martha Enriqueta Luján*

*Jeremy P. Tarcher/Putnam*
*a member of*
*Penguin Putnam Inc.*
*New York*

# THE ROAD TO
# GUADALUPE

## ERYK HANUT

### A MODERN PILGRIMAGE
### TO THE GODDESS
### OF THE AMERICAS

Most Tarcher/Putnam books are available at special quantity discounts for bulk purchases for sales promotions, premiums, fund-raising, and educational needs. Special books or book excerpts also can be created to fit specific needs. For details, write Putnam Special Markets, 375 Hudson Street, New York, NY 10014.

Jeremy P. Tarcher/Putnam
a member of
Penguin Putnam Inc.
375 Hudson Street
New York, NY 10014
www.penguinputnam.com

Library of Congress Cataloging-in-Publication Data

Hanut, Eryk, date.
    The road to Guadalupe : a modern pilgrimage to the goddess of the Americas / Eryk Hanut.
        p.    cm.
    ISBN 1-58542-120-0
        1. Guadalupe, Our Lady of—Miscellanea.    2. Mary, Blessed Virgin, Saint—Apparitions and miracles—Mexico—Guadalupe Hidalgo.
3. Mary, Blessed Virgin, Saint—Cult—Mexico.    4. Mexico—Religious life and customs.    I. Title.
BT660.G8 H38        2001                     2001026715
232.91'7'097253—dc21

Printed in the United States of America

10   9   8   7   6   5   4   3   2   1

This book is printed on acid-free paper. ♻

Book design by Deborah Kerner/Dancing Bears Design

To Andrew, for the best years of my life.


To Maria Todisco, the daughter of Saint George and Bonnie

Parker, who keeps things in Balance—and keeps

dragons and New Age flakes at bay.


To Bridget Bell, my first student and my timeless teacher.


To Purrball, Guadalupe's cat. We miss you every day.

*Con tu adiós, te llevas mi corazón.*

All of the dialogues in the following narrative of Her apparitions are taken from the *Nican Mopohua*. This short text is written in Nahuatl, the Aztec language, and its origins are as obscure, complex, and controversial as those of the Gospels. Some scholars attribute it to Don Antonio Valeriano (1520–1605), a nobleman who, according to legend, was related to the Aztec imperial family. Others believe it was written much later by Luis Lasso de la Vega, one of the first vicars of the Sanctuary of Guadalupe, the Ermita. It is likely no one will ever be certain of the name of its author or authors.

The manuscript was discovered in 1649, in the archives of the Ermita. It is the oldest testimony, and one of the most reliable, to the events of Guadalupe.

The narrative of the events is my invention. I wouldn't dare, of course, change a single line of the dialogues themselves. *Nican Mopohua* means "Here it is said."

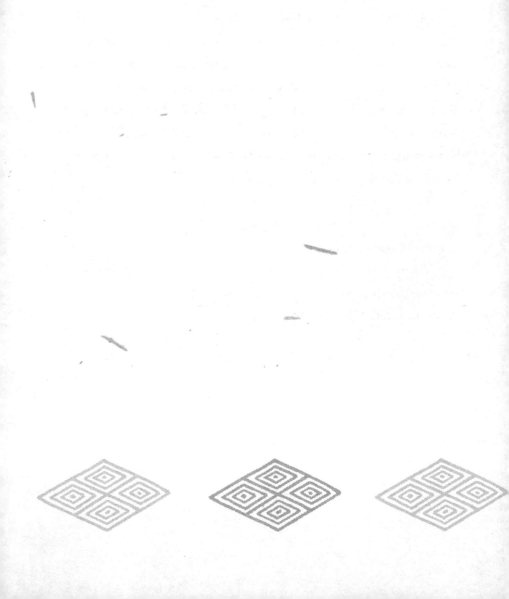

Mexico is a country built on its wounds.

—Carlos Fuentes

*Brujería:* A body of religious and folk magic practices that blends
Roman Catholicism and the Aztec goddess faith. It has been
influenced by other traditions, such as spiritism, Santería,
voodoo, Wicca, and ceremonial magic. It is common throughout
Mexico and among Chicano populations in the United States.
Practitioners are called *brujas* if female, and *brujos* if male,
although there appear to be few *brujos* in the United States.
*Brujería* is centered around the worship of Our Lady of
Guadalupe.

—adapted from *Dictionary of True Magic*

Mary is the unrecognized Mother Goddess of Christianity.

—Anne Baring

You can always find me in the less fortunate.

—Our Lady, in Banneux, Belgium, 1933

Landing at first light in Mexico City,

a land where nothing seems to grow.

Seen from the plane, through the tea-rose color of

 the perpetual smog,

the city seems to live in a perpetual dawn.

The brown land with its little lakes looks like

the pictures they took of the moon,

the moon where She rested her feet.

Or better yet, it looks like a magnified elephant skin. Yes, seen

 from a plane, Mexico looks like the bark of an old,

 dried-out, wrinkled elephant.

And it's down there She chose to come.

# THE ROAD TO GUADALUPE

It is a cold December morning; the sun has not yet risen. A short, squat man walks in the stark, desolate countryside, alone. He is heading to the church of Tlaltelolco, nine miles from his hamlet of Tolpetlac.

This man is one of the greatest unknowns of history. Very few things about him are clear. Some people have spent their lives digging through musty old libraries to find the parchment, the letter that would prove he *never* existed because nothing proves that he *ever* existed—nothing but a devotion strong as a tidal wave and an immense love, both of which, from a strictly scholarly point of view, mean nothing.

The little man's name is Juan Diego. He may be fifty-six or fifty-seven years old. But who really knows? Born Aztec, he is poor; his real name is supposed to have been Cuauhtlatóhuac. He converted to the new religion brought by the white man and was baptized ten years ago, receiving the unmistakably Christian name Juan Diego.

He may also be married or a widower. Some traditions grant him a María Lucía, perhaps dead, perhaps alive and well on this cold morning. In later times, the Catholic clergy, embarrassed by the idea of a saint in bed with his wife, will prefer him single and chaste and without any knowledge of the flesh. All we can be certain of is his name and his piety. My assertion that he is short is based on ethnic

1

facts, and also on his supposed age and circumstances. Poverty shrinks.

On this December morning, he is going to mass. The area around Tenochtitlán is gray and monotonous. The apparent absence of any form of life helps his spirit to wander and expand. Around him, nothing grows; nothing grows, after all, on an elephant's skin.

The world's largest metropolis, with approximately twenty-five million inhabitants. And surely the most polluted of all. For tourists, the smog has become a trademark of the city, a part of its identity, like bad manners in Paris.

*Será que hoy*
*el cielo con esmog*
*a mis espaldas me cayo*
*tome el reloj*
*y al escaparse de mis manos*
*simplemente se rompió.*

Sentimental songs (here by Armando Manzanero, a Mayan mixture of Tony Bennett and Judy Garland) refer to the smog the way songs in other countries mention breezes from the sea.

The green cabs, Volkswagen bugs, look like aphids in the traffic's running waters. The cabdriver taps obsessively on his wheel. A baby's shoe swings from the mirror. He repeats, *"Tráfico, tráfico . . ."* like a mantra against the evil spells of the road.

At a red light, lost in the middle of the *tráfico,* a big woman, badly made up as a clown, spits fire and swallows a sword. Her little girl begs, going from car to car, with hardly any success.

Andrew points toward a small grocery store on the left. Outside, an old woman sprinkles water on faded salads and leeks. I can hardly believe my eyes: It's called "O. J. Simpson Bazaar." The cab turns abruptly (like every car in Mexico) and streams into a long avenue. Each time I try to read its name, the cab speeds up; it's the Avenue of the Three-something. The façades of the houses are yellow, orange, baby blue, even fuchsia; they look as though they are in a vast, depressed game of Monopoly. In the middle of the avenue rear giant trees, swarming with violet trumpets. I've seen them before in India. And on the Place Furstemberg in Paris.

"Jacarandas," Andrew whispers. I had not known their name. I suddenly want to be a pedestrian, gathering their glowing petals.

An Aztec-inspired pyramid opens the Paseo de la Reforma. Our hotel is close now, in the Zona Rosa. "The exciting pink zone" is splashed in red letters over its stationery.

It's seven in the morning and the heat is already intense. In the car next to us, a woman with hair sculptured like one of the Supremes' applies bright coral lipstick. Her pink earrings resemble Bazooka bubble gum. I feel as if I'm in a film of Almodóvar.

The driver's mantra is now "Zona Rosa, Zona Rosa . . ." I long for him to shut up but, naturally, say nothing.

Policemen dressed like extras in an Offenbach operetta, with golden epaulettes lighting up their shoulders, whistle without conviction and to no effect on the anarchic traffic. The driver has now opened the window, so all the city's fumes engulf us, along with the klaxons, whistles, screeching arguments on the sidewalks, all blurred by the noise of traffic. And the driver, as if he were conducting it all, keeps muttering ". . . Zona Rosa, Zona Rosa . . ."

The hotel. At last. A monumental mansion in a calm street. Its doors open onto a huge staircase hung on both sides with portraits of sad-eyed prelates. At one time it was a bishop's palace. A first for me: Most of the time, the hotels where I've stayed have been former convents or brothels.

After a shower, we walk a few blocks and have breakfast.

### Breakfast

Very strong *café* (actually, hot milk with Nescafé)

*Huevos con carne*

*Pico de gallo*

Orange juice (smelling like mango juice; probably a
    badly rinsed glass)

Big pieces of fried bread

The waitress is fat and beautiful. She never smiles. Written in large black type underneath a vase of plastic carnations on our table is a sign: *Este hogar es católico. No aceptamos propaganda protestante ni de otras sectas. ¡Viva Cristo Rey! ¡Viva la Madre de Dios!* (This place is Catholic. We do not accept Protestant propaganda or that of other sects. Long live Christ the King! Long live the Mother of God!)

The restaurant's walls are melon colored. Among posters of Swiss lakes and puppies in straw baskets, a very beautiful but damaged *retablo,* represents the Holy Trinity. The beautiful fat girl is trying to repair a tape player with Scotch tape. The songs she half listens to are full of *"mi amor"* and *"corazón,"* as they are all around the world. Her repair efforts do not seem to be effective. She grabs the machine and shakes it close to her ear, as if it were a coconut. The singer's voice starts again, going from high soprano to a slow Chaliapin growl with a Betty Boop imitation in between.

While I pay her, I say to the girl—who hadn't asked—that we are here to see Guadalupe. She smiles briefly and crosses herself. The check is written on a tarot reader's business card. It mentions that she also reads tea leaves.

Then, for the next half-hour, despite my dreadful Spanish, I manage to learn from the waitress how to make *huevos con carne*.

### Huevos con Carne

1 tablespoon of olive oil (or clarified butter)

1 large onion, chopped (red onion's better)

3 cloves of garlic, chopped

3 large tomatoes, peeled and chopped

Salt and freshly ground black pepper

Pinch of brown sugar

2 green chiles, chopped

2 chorizo sausages, chopped and skinned

Cooked bacon—as much as you want

8 eggs, beaten

Tabasco sauce

Heat the oil in a skillet and sauté the onion and garlic until they turn translucent. Add tomatoes, salt and pepper, brown sugar, and chiles. Cook gently for five minutes. Add the sausages and bacon. Cook five more minutes. Add the eggs and cook over low heat, stirring with a wooden spoon—three to four minutes for a creamy consistency, five to six for a crispier result.

Season to taste with Tabasco sauce.

Serve with Corona beer—or any beer. White wine is good, too.

Totally nondiet. Wonderful.

Juan Diego approaches Tepeyac (or Tepeyacac) Hill. Before the arrival of the Spaniards, this hill was the place most sacred to the Aztecs. The shrine of the mother goddess Tonantzin was built here. *Tonantzin* is not really a name; it means simply "our mother." Another, even more reverential way the Aztecs addressed the divine feminine was *Totlaconantzin,* "our precious mother." Tonantzin (she has a lot of names) was the mother of all the gods in the Aztec pantheon. She was perpetually pregnant with all of them, and like the Asian Indian goddesses Kali or Durga, each and every aspect of Tonantzin mirrored another power of the sacred feminine. As the mother of fertility, she was called Cihuacoatl; under the name Tzinteotl, she was the protector of sexual ecstasy and prostitutes. From what we know of the Aztecs, it would be easy to imagine this place as a site of bloody sacrifice, although it is quite probable that Tonantzin never received anything but pigeons' and lambs' blood. However, among the Aztec deities, she was one of the gentlest.

Nothing, however, remains of her at Tepeyac on this morning in December 1531. Tepeyac is a round, dry hill in the middle of an area of large unhealthy lakes, near a city whose name isn't yet Mexico City. Perhaps a few ruined walls of her ancient temple straddle the rocks: No one can be sure today. When the Spaniards arrived, Bishop Zumárraga had all the idols and the temples of the pagans they had just invaded burned down. Despite the blood and ashes it has absorbed, the soil of

9

Tepeyac is not fertile; the conquerors cannot exploit it. So they leave it wild and abandoned. That's why, perhaps, the Indians love the area around Tepeyac. Everything is still the same; nothing much has changed. Stones, cacti, geckos, and poor people. A litany of species that can stand extremes.

In the taxi, en route to the basilica. We drive through poor neighborhoods. In one, naked children play with a water hose. Thank God for their wild laughter and leaping skinny brown bodies. I spot a beautiful orange sign above a store: *Azulejos*. In Portugal, the word refers to artistically painted blue-and-white tiles like the magnificent examples that cover Lisbon walls. Here it seems to refer to all kinds of tiles.

It must be nine A.M. by now. I try to remember what the smell of these streets awakens in me. It's a strong odor of gas fumes mingled with scorching dust, like on the road from Madras to Mahabalipuram in India years before. It was while working in a tremendously poor neighborhood that Saint Vincent de Paul concluded that poverty has no odor. Did his faith kill his sense of smell?

LA VILLA. It's the name of the sprawling, ugly, gigantic quarter where the two basilicas stand. The old one, closed in 1974, and the new one. Our white-haired, pot-bellied driver's name is Juan, but he prefers to be called John. He tells us so. He explains, *"La basílica . . .* going down, into the ground . . . Terrible, very bad." Each time he says "very bad," he touches his forehead. "Going down into the ground . . . Bad foundations [that lasted three hundred years] . . . because of the lakes . . . Then, they building a new *basílica* . . . Ugh!" He seems to be swallowing a bull's eye. "And when finished, the old *basílica* stopping sinking!" He turns to us, "Nuestra Señora not like her new house!"

I agree with the Blessed Mother. The new basilica is a gigantic concrete arena topped off by a kind of Godzilla-size scallop shell. Next to it, the old basilica, it's true, doesn't look very straight. Built in colonial baroque style, it is crowned by three turrets, one large, the other two smaller, all shiny like yellow onion skin. The fences erected around it don't for a moment discourage hordes of kids from running around inside the forbidden area. Seated on the old stairs, a group of pensive "little Rickys" stare out silently into the crowd with faces much older than their actual ages.

The first rosary dealers are installing their folding tables in the sun. Some sell only candles. Held in glass containers, they all bear the image of La Guadalupana. Smaller ones offer variations ("Guada" holding the Mexican flag). La Lupe, here she is, for all tastes, in all styles and sizes: small, large, made of glass, of plastic, turned into lamps, key rings, framed with seashells. There are outdoor virgins cast in resin, and glowing electric ones immersed in holy water. A large framed poster shows, from one angle, the image of La Lupe, and from another, the Pope. Roger, a plumber who was the fiancé of my aunt's cook in Paris, had a postcard of Raquel Welch, in a fur bikini, from *One Million Years B.C.* If you looked at it from the right, she would wink; look from the left, and she would blow you a kiss. I badgered him for months to give it to me. When he did, of course, the postcard instantly lost its magic.

Old men cross the place, arms loaded with chains, medals, rosaries. *"Cinco pesos, dos por cinco pesos."*

The Villa is squeezed between two highways and surrounded by tall, orange-painted grilles. If you come from the west, you have to take a bridge that crosses above the traffic. As in a Latin American version of Benares, groups of cripples and beggars wait for you: They have probably spent the night there. A child kneeling in the middle of the path scratches a zither. The hand he uses is fingerless, as if he had worn it down by always playing the same sour note. *"Pesopesopeso..."* The same word echoes from everywhere at regular intervals. One peso is the price of a cheap rosary, of an ice cream sandwich, or a key ring from Taiwan.

Large canvases hang from the orange grilles. Naïve and violently colored, with Nuestra Señora, and Juan Diego at her feet. Near the canvases, a photographer waits, armed with an old Polaroid camera. When he succeeds at stopping tourists—which is infrequent—he poses them against the wall with the holy background behind. If you tip him well, he'll insist on placing you just underneath the Virgin's downcast eyes so you receive an instant blessing. On some of the canvases, Guada wears a ribbon like a beauty-pageant queen, *"Recuerdo de La Villa"* streaked across it in gold letters. When children have their pictures taken, they sit on a life-size green-and-red plastic donkey with chipped ears, its head wreathed with moth-eaten artificial carnations.

Suddenly, a sugary smell surrounds me. On the side of the grille, a large woman hands me a small pastry; it's very hot, with no specific taste except sweetened flour. *"Gorditas,"* she says, smiling. She rolls these, ten at a time, in colorful paper cylinders and stacks them in a pyramid near her frying pan. The woman next to her is also frying *gorditas,* but she patriotically wraps them only in green, red, or white paper. She stirs the fresh dough with one hand while chasing away the sparrows that cluster around her with the other.

In less than fifteen minutes, the sleepy place has become alive, like a film begun in slow motion that has found its real speed. An old man sells images framed with aloe leaves and garlic cloves pierced with nails. Witchcraft doesn't seem far away. Now the whole plaza is covered with the same spiritual junk. The Virgin is no longer alone; a battalion of saints has joined her on the camping tables: Saint Judas Tadeo, Saint Martin of Porres, Saint Thérèse of Lisieux, all of them richly decorated with sequins, gold strings, blue-glass stars. Paradise by Bob Mackie.

I find Andrew bargaining with a rosary dealer. She is about fifty years old and can translate "rosary" into innumerable languages. The large doors of the new basilica are wide open. From a distance, the sounds of the beginning mass flow to us. "No, no!" shrieks the rosary specialist. She snatches back the one I picked and closes my palm on another. Then she opens it and brings it under my nose. *"Rosa, rose, fleur . . ."* The rosary smells of rose, of rose soap. She gestures toward the inside of the church, *"La Señora . . . rosa, rosa."* She seems to want to say that Guadalupe herself came to sprinkle her rosaries with a heavenly fragrance. She must see she is winning. The red cinnamon beads are beautiful. She picks up a crucifix from her table and puts it against my eye. After a few seconds, I can see through a tiny aperture the Virgin bathed in Chartres blue.

I give in and nod; she is thrilled. *"Nuestra Señora de Guadalupe,"* she announces proudly. Now that the Virgin and I have been introduced to each other, in a way, I feel I can walk into the shrine. But the woman doesn't seem to want to part so fast. She fetches out of a worn black velvet bag heavy silver bracelets, much too shiny to be real. "Medallions, bracelets . . . made by prisoners. My father was a prisoner . . . *Parlez-vous français?* . . . The war, bad, very bad . . . Very cheap bracelets . . . You have dollars?"

Juan Diego carries on walking. Today is December 9; yesterday was the Feast of the Immaculate Conception. Is he aware of it? Almost certainly not. As he reaches the top of the hill, he hears a strange sound, a kind of music, the *Nican Mopohua* tells us, "as if different precious birds were singing and their song would alternate, as if the hill was answering them." It must have been astounding to this simple man. The text has him exclaiming in wonder, "By chance do I deserve this? Am I worthy of what I am hearing? Maybe I am dreaming? Maybe I only see this in my dreams? Maybe I am in the land of my ancestors, of the elders, of our grandparents? In the Land of Flower, in the earth of our flesh? Maybe over there inside of heaven?"

From somewhere he hears a voice calling him, "Dignified Juan Diego." A voice that calls him "dignified"? He, whose race has been massacred in the name of a blond god of love? He, whose people now wander aimlessly in alcoholism and depression? He, of the race whose raped women have no other solution but to kill their children to avoid watching them starve? How could he be dignified?

The strange "thing" is now only a few steps away. During the first apparitions in Lourdes, Bernadette would call the Lady *aguerro,* "thing" in Pyrenean dialect.

It's a young, very young woman. She seems to be fourteen or fifteen. Her skin is dark. Her face, even though lovely, is swollen, a sign that she is about to give birth. She shows, under her breasts, the *cinta,* a black ribbon with which she is saying, *"Estoy encinta"* (I am pregnant). She wears an emerald coat covered with gold stars and, underneath, a pale pink dress.

When he arrived in her presence, he marveled at her perfect beauty. Her clothing appeared like the sun, and it gave forth rays. And the rock and the cliffs where she was standing, upon receiving the rays like arrows of light, appeared like precious emeralds, appeared like jewels: The earth glowed with the splendors of the rainbow. The mesquites, the cacti, and the weeds that were all around appeared like feathers of the quetzal, and the stems looked like turquoise; the branches, the foliage, and even the thorns sparkled like gold.

The light is so blinding that Juan Diego cannot decide if it's coming from her or from a second sun rising behind her. No, it's coming from her, from underneath her skin. She says, "Listen, my most abandoned son, dignified Juan. Where are you going?" And here, it's certain, Juan Diego falls to his knees.

Unconsciously, Andrew and I are hesitant to walk inside the basilica. We've been turning around the building for half an hour now. We've gone outside the orange grilles, the border that limits the Villa's territory. A symbolic border, because the misery and the number of beggars is the same in and out.

I hold a small statue of Guadalupe in my hand. "Eight pesos." The dark bearded man shows me other models. "This one, ten pesos, better." The ten-peso version has a glittering red dress. The glitter sticks to my hand after I put it back. I remark that, on the table next to him, the same statues are four pesos.

"Yes," he says, "but mine are blessed by the bishop. Much better."

We finally penetrate the new basilica, arms full of votives, which are already melting. The inside of the building is a covered arena. If it weren't for the large crucifix in the center, it could be a rock concert stadium, or a massive surgical amphitheater, or a convention center. Women in gray aprons with yellow badges on their breasts are mopping the immense floors with towels much bigger than themselves. Like the Golden Gate Bridge, the Basilica of Guadalupe is washed and cared for all day long, all year long. One of the cleaning women close to us sings a rock song, and between lyrics, mumbles amens to the priests who celebrate mass.

The new sanctuary was built in the mid seventies and inaugurated in 1976. It can hold up to ten thousand seated pilgrims; not that many, if you think of the three to four million people who come here for the big pilgrimage in December.

This morning, there are around two thousand people, mostly women, of all ages and classes. Bejeweled old María Félix types sit next to white-haired, raisin-faced peasant women with hands gnarled by work. And young mothers. Hundreds of young mothers and hundreds of babies, many of them newborn, wrapped in flowing white shawls.

As we walk in, two women are getting ready for the first ritual of their pilgrimage. They kneel at the door and walk forward on their knees to the first row of chairs, holding lighted candles and rocking to and fro. It's about one hundred yards. I get to my knees too and follow them—the hardest one hundred yards of my life.

A little girl is with them, extremely agitated and determined to have her mother (or her sister—mothers in Mexico can be very young or old) in her normal standing position. She starts to scream. No one cares. Her voice joins the priests' and the *"Pesopesopeso"* chant that follows you everywhere around La Villa, and sweeps into the immense vessel with the waves of hot air, carrying smells of frying *gorditas,* car fumes, and dust.

The Tilma is at the end of the basilica, framed in gold and silver. I've been trying to avoid looking in its direction. If there weren't so many people on line to the relic, I would walk with my eyes closed and open them just in front of her.

The Tilma (it's feminine; it's La Tilma) hangs on the central wall of the building at the base of an enormous wooden structure shaped like a large lung in the center of the basilica. Enormous silver chandeliers, looking like jellyfish, seem to float around it.

I am still quite far away, but the Tilma appears smaller than in my expectations, as if things that change the course of history should be gigantic in size.

The mass is ending; another will start immediately. This goes on all day long, just like the church cleaning. The faithful swarm against a wood fence around the choir to receive blessing and holy water spread by a hawk-faced, pimply young priest who seems stunned with boredom. The booming organ stops for a moment, the human tide ebbs, and spreading in all directions is another almost pleasant smell: a mixture of frankincense, armpits, and ripe cut flowers. The perfume of the Basilica of Guadalupe.

Juan Diego is scared. The apparition speaks Nahuatl, the Aztec language, his ancestors' language. Nevertheless, he answers, "My owner and my queen, I have to go to the Church of Tlaltelolco, to follow the divine things that our priests, who are the image of Our Lord, give to us."

The lady says, "Know and be certain in your heart, my most abandoned son, that I am the Ever Virgin Holy Mary, Mother of the God of Great Truth, Teotl, of the one through whom we live, the creator of persons, the owner of what is near and together, of the Lord of heaven and earth."

She continues, "I want very much that my hermitage be erected in this place. In it, I will show and give to all people all my love and compassion, my help and my protection, because I am your merciful mother and the mother of all nations that live on this earth who would love me and who place their confidence in me. There I will hear their laments and remedy and cure all their miseries, misfortunes, and sorrows. And for this merciful wish of mine to be realized, go there to the palace of the bishop of Mexico, and you will tell him in what way I have sent you to be my messenger, so that you may make known to him I very much desire that he build me a home right here, that he may erect my temple on the plain. You will tell carefully everything you have seen and admired and heard.

"Be absolutely certain that I will make you joyful, I will repay you. I will give you happiness, and you will earn much that will repay you for your trouble and your work in carrying out what I have entrusted to you. Look, my son, the most abandoned one, you have heard my statement and my word. Now, do everything that relates to you."

Juan Diego bows his head. What else can he do? He answers, "My owner and my queen, I am already on the way to make your statement and your word a reality. And now, I depart from you, I, poor servant." And the little man runs to the bishop's palace as fast as he can.

One of the day's interminable masses is ending. There is not much difference in the behavior of the faithful before, during, and after mass. I've only once before witnessed such pious anarchy, in Mahabalipuram, in south India, where, during a Ganesh festival, the appearance of the elephant god, wreathed in pink-and-yellow robes, aroused screams and whistles as wild as those that greet Mick Jagger.

During mass, the pilgrims of Guadalupe get up, talk to each other, wander from one row of benches to another, breast-feed babies quite openly, but all without ever losing their naked devotion. Anywhere else in the world, such an attitude would seem profane. Not here. Here, it seems brattily peaceful, the way kittens play around their mother.

A priest points out to us the place where we can see the Tilma close up. To get there, you need to walk down an impressive gray marble staircase behind the main altar.

Four moving walkways come and go underneath the altar, invisible to the crowd that faces the altar, in an enclosure like an open crypt. The Tilma is hung against the gold and wooden wall, about eight feet above eye level, placed so expertly that it can be seen from every angle. The walkways are like those you see in airports, but shorter. Like most of the automated machines in Mexico City, they need oil or repair. They sound sometimes like squeaking babies' voices; most of the time they make a bizarre buzz, like that of spirits crossing over from one world to another in B horror movies. It is as if all the suffering cries and complaints of the world were rising up to the Virgin in the Tilma; all the world's misery that begs for relief seems to be hidden in the creaking of the badly oiled escalators.

At last I raise my eyes. They fill with tears. Looking down below, looking at me, looking at each and every face, is the Mother of the True God Teotl, who printed her own image on a piece of cloth long ago. A cactus cloth; cloth from a cactus called maguey. It's from the sap of the same plant that tequila is distilled. How strange and marvelous that Guadalupe and tequila, the two pillars that have sustained Mexico for so long, helping it through the dark, spring from the same plant.

La Tilma is, as I said, enclosed by two frames. The one that surrounds the image directly is of pure gold; the larger one is silver. The freshness of the image itself, its colors, are indescribable. I have read about this quality in many books; I thought it Catholic propaganda, but it's astonishingly true. It's the color of her coat that strikes me. It's pine, light emerald, like that of a Caribbean lagoon. What also strikes me is how small the Tilma is. It measures only sixty-six by forty-one inches. Juan Diego must have been so short. The maguey fiber should have turned to dust hundreds of years ago. It was a fabric used only by poor people who couldn't afford wool, let alone silk. Usually, maguey doesn't last longer than twenty years.

I am at last facing the most famous miraculous relic in the world, along with the Holy Shroud of Turin, and I find I cannot pray. Dozens of people—women and men of all ages—float by under the Tilma. Some raise their hands, filled with rosaries or icons or flickering candles, hoping that La Lupe will understand and bless them first.

To the side of the escalator a couple waits. They look desperate and lost. He is short, square, with the thick bushy mustache you see in the photographs of Pancho Villa. She has the gaze of someone drowning and carries a crying baby wrapped in a violet blanket. She's seven or eight months pregnant. Her belly protrudes from the red satin baseball jacket she's wearing, wrongly buttoned up. Is it his? The couple seem to be hesitating; before they get onto the escalator, they look each other over silently, as if to make sure they have counted all their requests, all their wounds, and that now they are ready to go.

The smell of hot wax starts to disturb me. Next to me, there's a father and his baby boy. The father is much younger than I. He takes the supple arm of the child and sketches the sign of the cross with it in the air. Near him, an old woman takes the rosary she was holding up and puts it on the baby, who starts to scream as if possessed.

Above us, the men of God have started another mass. The main voice repeats, from time to time, *"Santa María de Guadalupe,"* like a blasé waiter announcing tonight's specials.

I want some fresh air. At the door, an old nun, like a fat and wrinkled mastiff that just woke up, waits for the pilgrims with a basketful of images. I put a dollar in the basket and take an image. "No!" She violently takes back her image and looks somewhere else, as if I weren't there. I feel hurt, as if I have been slapped.

Outside, among the merchants of the temple, I see a beautiful tall woman who looks at me, smiling; I recognize her from her skirt with its huge orange flowers and her bright pink lipstick: She was in the line to the Tilma with us. "She didn't want to give you an image," she says, "because she saw that your candles hadn't been bought at the basilica's store. Welcome to the Basilica of Guadalupe!" she laughs. Then, looking down at the shrunken figure of the nun, she feigns to spit in her direction. She laughs again. *"Puta!"*

The *tilma* was a very common piece of clothing for the Aztecs. As in most ethnic traditions, the way you wore it and the fabric it was made of revealed the class you were from. The privileged class wore *tilmas* woven from cotton, most of the time undyed: The pure white one was reserved for holy festivals. The rich wore theirs attached on the right shoulder, either folded back or pinned by a sort of fibula. The middle and low classes would have agave or maguey *tilmas,* fixed on the left shoulder. The poorest would display their *tilmas* fastened on the back of the neck, a sign that they were unemployed and were looking for jobs as porters or servants.

The Tilma of Guadalupe is, in fact, divided into two pieces of maguey fiber, sewn together in the middle. It is quite probable that the original cloth was bigger and was cut by some sixteenth-century zealots to fit the frame.

Like the Shroud of Turin, the Tilma has been the prey of scientists for the last century; unlike the Shroud of Turin, nobody has ever explained or demystified it. Back in 1666, the first documented commission, made up of painters and art masters, unanimously declared the piece "a miracle," adding that "a beauty and countenance so modestly joyful is humanly inimitable."

I've mentioned earlier that the life expectancy of maguey fiber is no more than twenty years, in ideal circumstances. After that, the fiber turns into dust and disappears. In the case of the Tilma of the Virgin of Guadalupe, however, the image is imprinted on a still totally intact material that was, for more than one hundred years, displayed without any frame or protective glass. The Tilma was not only the victim of changes of temperature, but also of votives that burned night and day, depositing layers of carbon monoxide everywhere; besides, no rules, back then, forbade the children to kiss the image of their mother. Just observe the dark smudges an occasional candle leaves on white walls and you soon realize that the astonishing condition the Tilma is itself a kind of miracle.

A letter written in 1753 and kept in The Mexico City Library mentions that its author, in less than two hours, had witnessed the Tilma's being touched with more than five hundred different objects, from rosaries to baby clothes.

In 1791, two locksmiths, while cleaning the silver frame, accidentally poured nitric acid on the cloth. No damage was observed, just a light stain. The metal frame, however, was ravaged.

Better yet, in 1921, during the persecutions of the Catholic Church by the regime, an anarchist left a bomb hidden in a vase of roses at the feet of the Virgin in the old shrine. It exploded at the end of a service, damaging walls and marble bas-reliefs. A procession cross, made of gold and heavy copper, melted like caramel in the blaze; it is still on display in a window in the basilica, lying on a rich red velvet pillow that follows its twisted, agonized curve. The Tilma was unharmed. Only after the attack did church authorities decide to enclose the Tilma in bulletproof glass, behind which it is still sheltered today.

In 1936, two fragments of the maguey cloth were sent to Germany to be examined by Professor Richard Kuhn, winner of a Nobel Prize in chemistry, at the Kaiser Wilhelm Institute in Heidelberg. His diagnosis shook the scientific world. He confessed later that before the tests, the idea of unveiling a four-hundred-year-old religious hoax had been a thrilling one. Yet he wrote that "the elements that produce the colored patches on the cloth are unknown to all research. Neither mineral, animal, nor vegetable, the image seems to have been painted without any brush stroke or lithographic method."

Further examination in Mexico in 1946, by a strongly atheist team, could not defeat Dr. Kuhn's conclusions. Even if the 1946 team was cautious about using the word "miracle," their verdict was clear: "If the image of the woman on the cloth had been hand made, it could have only been made by techniques unknown by artists and scientists of the twentieth century." Meanwhile, they observed meticulously that the rays of light surrounding the Virgin were painted in oil, as was the angel at the bottom of the image. When seen through a microscope, the texture of these parts of the Tilma was totally different. They also noted for the record that the fingers of the Lady seemed to have been shortened by a painter, perhaps to make her more characteristically Aztec in appearance.

The best, most convincing, and strangest, however, was yet to come. Back in 1929, a photographer variously cited as Alfonso González and Alfonso Marcué claimed that a human face could be seen in an enlarged close-up of the eye of the Virgin. Twenty-two years later, in 1951, a group of photographers developed close-ups of extravagant sizes that would indeed reveal figures in the iris of the Mother of God. Some have counted more than seventeen people in one eye, the most famous being, of course, a little kneeling figure identified as Juan Diego. A dark-skinned feminine figure that can also be seen clearly is considered the black servant of Zumárraga mentioned in several contemporary records.

Of course, you can play games like this for hours. Finding faces or figures in passing clouds or the shapes of rocks is nothing new. Still, the incredible fact is that the figures are reflected on a convex angle, as if by a lens or an eye. No painter could have conceived this. Dozens of ophthalmologists in the sixties and seventies went to work on the enigma without coming up with any convincing answers. In the late seventies, the eyes of the Virgin of Guadalupe were scrutinized by a rigorous team of scientists from Florida State University. One of them, Dr. Philip Callahan, declared that "studying the Tilma was the most strange and the most moving thing in my life. It is probable that we'll never know who painted the Tilma, and how it was made; there is actually no human explanation. You can break life down into atoms, but what comes after that? Even Einstein said 'God.'"

Recently, astronomers from Mexico City University created a transparency of the map of the sky as it was on December 12, 1531, the day of the creation of the image on the Tilma. When they laid out the transparency on an exact copy of the Tilma, they were stunned to discover that the stars on the coat matched their astral chart exactly. Even more suggestively, when a transparency of the Tilma was laid out on a topographical map of central Mexico, it was found that the map's mountains, lakes, and rivers were mirrored precisely in the decorations on Guadalupe's robes.

Back at the hotel, I ask the receptionist in the lobby what he thinks of the Tilma. Does he believe it to be authentic? Like most of the Mexicans I've met so far, he crosses himself at the mention of the image. "No man could have painted it," he almost whispers. "It's like a Polaroid taken by God."

Before my encounter with the raw force of Mexico City, I had a tame, saccharine image of what the hill of Tepeyac would be like—dry, very Alice Springs, calm and distant, with white desert sanctuaries and the only movement the flickering flames of votive candles and two or three old ladies in black, carrying dozens of carnations.

The real, very different Tepeyac is located just behind the noisy sprawl of La Villa. The wild hill of the *Nican Mopohua* has been domesticated and transformed into a campy park with brilliant green lawns and water conduits in the shape of jaguar mouths. Gigantic gray staircases, crowned by gaudy arches of bougainvillea and wisteria, wind you slowly to its summit, El Cerrito, the site of the chapel where Juan Diego is buried.

Near a group of statues of La Madre, Juan Diego, and some Aztec warriors (what are they doing here?), is planted a straggly rose garden. The sign says it's been offered by the city of Sacramento, California. At each shadowed spot on the route, the same photographer seems to lurk. With the same painted backdrop and the same blank-eyed resin donkey, their Guadalupes gaze up, as if they don't care about what's going on and long for heaven's peace.

To the right, past a gallery of stores brimming over with the usual religious kitsch and some monstrous jars of colored water, there extends an extremely Victorian-looking cemetery, the Panteón de Tepeyac. It looks like some of the more over-the-top areas of Highgate

Cemetery in London, with its tall, half-naked Apollos and weeping angels draped with poinsettias.

"Eh, you!" A woman's voice stops me in front of the chapel itself. I am ready to say no, as I've said many times in the last two hours, to the tarot reader, the rosary dealer, the flower girl, the cake girl, the candle girl. . . .

This woman is squat and robust, around forty years old, with a red T-shirt, short-cropped auburn hair, and a sharp-nosed face scarred with acne. "I recognized you! You were in the plane from Phoenix yesterday, no? I recognized your accent!"

She shakes my hand vigorously. "I am Maria." I say, "That's an appropriate name here," but her absence of any reaction shows me it was a stupid remark. I ask her if she is on a pilgrimage. She seems surprised. "My parents left Mexico City for the States when I was seven. I grew up in a barrio near L.A. When I was a kid, all my parents' friends were Mexican. Everybody had La Virgen on the fireplace. Her, and the Sagrado Corazón. They would listen to Vikki Carr and do parties. The Madre, she is a part of my life." She adds, "Each time I stop in Mexico City, I come and say hello to her. I say 'Hi, Madre!' "

She does not understand what Andrew and I are doing here. "Mexico City? Crazy, dreadful place . . . You should go to Cancún! To Acapulco, now that's real great! But here? Nothing to do. You are not going to spend all your time with the Madre?" She looks at us both as if we were half mad. Then Maria tells us that she has a business in Vegas (we'll never know what type of business), but she is in Mexico to get medical care.

"My teeth! U.S. sooooo expensive!"

Behind her, fountains carved into the walls spit water. Some Aztec divinities, among them Quetzalcoatl, the feathered snake. Tepeyac has been turned into a Petit Trianon, manicured and polished, but they've kept some of the old guard. Out of respect for Tonantzin, perhaps. Or fear.

Maria chatters away now, linking arms with us.

"My grandmother, no, my great-grandmother, she was a kind of *curandera* . . . a white witch . . . She's dead. She would transfer your sickness into an egg and throw the egg in the river. Too bad she's dead, you would have loved her. She was wild."

A purple bell flower from a jacaranda tree falls on her cheek; she jumps, screams, and then laughs at herself. "Oh, good . . . I thought it was a bee or a bug. Here, everything has a sting!"

I tell her the name of the tree, which I learned the day before. She smiles. "I've spent forty-two years of my life without knowing it. I've called it 'the blue tree' all my life. Should I change?"

"No," I tell her. " 'Blue tree' is beautiful."

Maria checks nervously at her wristwatch. *"Hasta luego, muchachos."* Then, looking us over, a couple of men, she takes a sharp breath and plunges. "You know," she speaks slowly, "I am a lesbian." Growing up lesbian in a barrio near L.A.—God knows she must know a few tricks about survival. "La Virgen, she accepts everybody. It's the Church that spreads bullshit. But the Virgin, she takes everybody in. Didn't she say to Juan Diego, 'Are you not in the hollow of my mantle where I cross my arms?' "

We stand looking calmly into each other's eyes. She repeats softly, "She takes everybody in." This time, I shake her hand first. "I've always known that, but it's good to be reminded. Thank you for reminding us." She keeps my hand a second in hers. *"Hasta luego, caballeros.* Eh, we exchanged informations!" She points her finger toward the mauve branches of the tree arching over us both: "What's the name again? Zadaranda?"

The bishop, Juan de Zumárraga, had arrived in the New World four years before, in 1527. Born in Basque country in 1468 (his birth date is not certain; some documents give it as 1470), Zumárraga felt attracted to the priesthood from an early age. From 1520 to 1523, it is almost certain that he was a Franciscan priest in the province of Durango, Spain. In 1523, Emperor Charles V named him inquisitor in the witchcraft and heresy trials. We know few things about him from that period: It's probably better that way, considering his task. In 1527, the emperor chose him as Bishop of the New World. One of his titles was Protector of the Indians. Zumárraga is said to have been patient and indulgent with the natives. But these records were written by Franciscans, so it is hard to rely on their objectivity. An ex-inquisitor must have been tough on people for whom human sacrifice was considered quite normal.

A few years later, in 1542, the king of Spain created a committee designed to protect the natives and to listen to their requests and complaints. His intentions might have been sincere, but one can't help shivering, thinking of similar committees set up in South Africa during apartheid.

But let's go back to Juan Diego. He is running to the bishop's palace in Tenochtitlán (now Mexico City). There he asks to speak with Bishop Zumárraga. (This would be as easy as for a beggar today to walk into the White House and demand a private audience with the president.)

Zumárraga must be slightly intrigued from the beginning, because the *Nican Mopohua* tells us that Juan Diego is asked to wait for hours. His Eminence finally shows up and listens to the little man's tale. He is with a translator, of course; Juan Diego speaks only Nahuatl. What are these three people thinking and feeling? Finally the bishop sends Juan Diego away. "My son, you will come another time and I will calmly listen to you. I have to see from the beginning the reason you have come and your will and your wish."

Here is an interesting moment. If we believe the *Nican Mopohua,* and there's no reason not to, Zumárraga is kind to the frightened man, a fact unusual enough to be commented on. Juan Diego must, nevertheless, have been sad. A feeling he knew well, probably. He left for his village by the road to Tepeyac.

And then there is the name beneath the name. Nowhere in the *Nican Mopohua* does the apparition call herself Guadalupe. Another version of the events of Tepeyac, titled *Inin Huey Tlamahuizoltzin* (This is the great wonder), and possibly predating the *Nican Mopohua,* ignores the appellation Guadalupe entirely.

So where does the name come from, and why is it used in this way? The name Guadalupe is from Spain; there is a sanctuary of Our Lady of Guadalupe in the south of Spain. The Basilica of Guadalupe— the other Guadalupe—is located in Cáceres, in the province of Estremadura. The surrounding landscapes strangely evoke those around Mexico City; they have the same dryness, but there, the proximity of the sierra and the absence of industry keep the population in a dignified poverty, and the skies are clear of smog.

The Spanish Guadalupe is a Black Madonna made of wood. In one arm she holds the infant Jesus, and in the other, a scepter made of gold and quartz. According to legend, the statue was offered by Saint Gregory the Great to the bishop of Seville, around the year 580. When the Moors invaded Spain at the beginning of the eighth century, the statue disappeared. Some faithful monks had hidden it in the woods. They hid it so well that it was lost for six hundred years. It would be found by a cowherd looking for his lost cow. A lady ringed with light appeared to him and indicated with her hand the direction of the village of Guadalupe (literally, "wolf's river," or even "the waters of the wolf"). A little later, the statue was discovered intact in a cave.

The king, Alfonso XI, commanded that a fortress-monastery be built to protect the precious relic. For several hundred years, she became *la favorita de España*. Columbus is said to have had a great devotion to the statue: He was carrying an image of her when he landed in the New World. A year later, in 1493, while sailing to the island of Karukera, his ship escaped a violent storm. Thanking his heavenly patron, and as an act of inspired imperialism, he rebaptized the island Guadalupe.

It is extremely unusual to be able to see the statue naked, without any ornaments; along with her look-alike in Chartres and so many other black madonnas, she is nearly always covered with velvet, lace, and jewels, whose arrangement changes with every feast day.

But how and why and when did the Lady of Mexico City inherit the other's name? The first missionaries tried to spread the cult of the

Mother of God as much as they could: It was the New Spain after all. The name *Guadalupe* cannot be spelled in Nahuatl because the letters *d* and *g* don't exist in the Aztec alphabet. And the girl from Tepeyac does not correspond to the description of the Spanish Virgin. So why, then, does the New World call her that?

The most probable theory is that she introduced herself under a name that *sounded* like "Guadalupe," but wasn't. And then Zumárraga understood—or chose to understand—that she was Guadalupe. The Indians had a hard time calling the lady who had appeared to one of them by a Spanish name. They had already suffered greatly from the Spaniards, so to call an apparition of the Virgin that had appeared to one of their own by a Spanish name must have been one more cruel humiliation.

A codex dated from the end of the sixteenth century mentions that "It is forbidden to call the shrine of Our Lady of Guadalupe 'the house of Tonantzin' or other pagan names; the ones that will do so will be fined."

Recent research asserts that the name heard by Juan Diego was probably Coatlaxopeuh or Tequantlaxopeuh (teh-keht-uh-LO-peh), which means "the one who triumphs over the rule of the serpent." A wonderful theory, much more appealing to me than the one of a borrowed name. "The one that triumphs over the rule of the serpent" is still adored completely in her basilica, despite the patriarchal rituals that are performed all day. In the presence of her worshippers, it doesn't take long to realize that Guadalupe is the last Goddess.

As I'm coming down Tepeyac Hill, too crowded for a first visit, just at
the bottom of the monumental staircase I spot a small church in the
Islamic style, with beautiful steeples of blue tiles. It's the baptistery,
also called Iglesia Santa María de Guadalupe. (What else?)

Inside the church is a holy well. Tradition has it that years after the
apparitions, Juan Diego and Zumárraga were taking a walk around
the Ermita. When the bishop asked him the exact spot of the last apparition, Juan Diego hesitated for a moment and looked around; he
couldn't remember precisely. He didn't have time to regret his amne-
sia too long, however, because nearby a spring suddenly burst out from
the ground. Juan easily identified it as marking the place where the
last visit of the Lady had occurred.

And so, just as in Lourdes, Banneux, La Salette, and other Marian
or pagan goddess sites, the spring, symbol of purification (and also of
fertility in this torrid climate) has been curing and relieving pain for the
last five hundred years. As Peggy Streep writes in *Sanctuaries of the
Goddess:* "The sacrality of water in the religion of the Goddess begins
in the Paleolithic . . . Water as divine moisture remained part of the sacred sites connected to the Goddess, connected to her role as life-giver
and chthonic power."

The well is located just inside the entrance of the church, covered
with a rusty black iron grille: It is, of course, forbidden to take water
from it. The water is for sale in every store around, bottled in

Guadalupe-shaped flasks of all sizes, with the Virgin's crown for a cork.

The maid of the hotel told me that only the descendants of Juan Diego are permitted by ancestral rights to make business with the well water. The abundance of bottles all around, however, leaves you skeptical about the capacity of this humble well (even for a miraculous spring, it seems prodigious) and also about the fertility of Juan Diego's family who, if the sources are to be believed, had no children.

Inside the church, there's a ceiling bursting with Rubenesque cherubs—blond, blue-eyed, and potbellied—that would be more appropriate somewhere in Bavaria. The Savior in wax, with a ferociously realistic ravaged face, lies in agony in a glass coffin where his head turns beseechingly toward you. The glass is covered with greasy finger marks, lipstick traces, the blood of red carnations rubbed by pilgrims ceaselessly against the reliquary till they look like shredded raw beef.

Outside, I start to look for a toilet. Furiously. As always around the Villa, if you're not buying something, nobody knows anything. I catch sight of a nun whom I had seen this morning—more heard than seen, because her laughter was quite hysterical, nearly scary, with the fixed eyes of a nurse that could strangle elderly patients while continuing to laugh. She indicates the direction of the toilets. "You need to walk about three hundred yards, then turn on the right; couldn't be simpler." And she laughs again even more crazily.

In a small, crooked, deserted street, I finally catch the WC sign. A squat, bewhiskered little man looking like Sergeant García leans against the wall. *"Dos pesos,"* he croaks. After I pay, he pushes me inside and closes the door fast behind me as if afraid the bathroom genie will leave. I find myself in a long gray corridor like that of a slum school, with peeling walls. At the end of it looms a large rotunda with a filthy glass dome. In its center is a dry fountain filled with dusty, faded silk flowers. From the glass dome itself hangs a mirrored sphere, stolen, it looks like, from a long-deceased disco: Small pieces of shattered mirror lie scattered on the floor. After pushing at several doors, all locked, I finally find the toilets. In the tiny room, a giant garish Guadalupe soars on the wall above two toilet bowls placed next to each other.

In the shuddering, flimsy taxi back to the hotel, I remember that it was in Paris where I first heard the name of Guadalupe and first saw an image of the Tilma.

In my early twenties, I would often visit Monsieur Diaz, an antique book dealer who had a small, plush gallery in the Palais Royal. He was the first Mexican person I had ever met and talked to. Monsieur Diaz was more than eighty years old then, handsome and dry like a wooden *santero;* or, to put it more prosaically, he looked like Cesar Romero. Spindly and extremely tall, always impeccably dressed in gray or pearly Japanese designer suits, he played Mozart sonatas on his antique blond Pleyel piano installed in the center of his boutique. He wouldn't stop or even look up if he decided the visitors that had pushed open his door didn't suit his space. I remember he coughed a lot, dramatically, and would take his medicines in a large gold spoon he swore came from *la vieille Russie.*

I don't know when Monsieur Diaz left Mexico. Long, long ago, undoubtedly, because his French was flawless, with just a soft purr in it, like a breeze. But even that came more from emphysema, perhaps, than from his Mexican origins.

He had spent time in Hollywood in the twenties; not long, but long enough to break Ramon Novarro's heart. In the thirties in Berlin he had shared a house with an old man who had been one of the few to follow Oscar Wilde's pauper's coffin to his first borrowed grave. Since he had known famous people from the neighborhood who had died forty years before, it was safe to call Monsieur Diaz a *parisien d'origine.*

He hardly ever mentioned Mexico in his conversations. Yes, only once he had said, "We didn't have any mosquitoes in our house in Durango. Not a single one; my mother wouldn't ever have allowed it."

One day, under the pretense of showing me some drawings of Forrain, Monsieur Diaz opened the door of a small antechamber adjoining the boutique. There, among some treasures and the unavoidable gouache Italian boys of Baron Corvo, was a large, unusual image of Guadalupe carved on a piece of leather. I asked Monsieur Diaz who she was, and he replied simply, *"La Reina."* Then he smiled, showing beautiful teeth that were obviously fake, and added, *"C'est la patronne"*—She's the boss.

Monsieur Diaz was a hard drinker; not a drunk. He would mix a green liquor, probably absinthe, with hot, black tea. He also knew the recipe for a Mexican cocktail called *Por mi amante,* which took you "high, very fast."

One afternoon, he wrote out the recipe on the back of a yellowing postcard of Colette in bed, surrounded by cats and paperweights. I still have it.

### Por Mi Amante

> 2 pounds fresh strawberries, sliced
> Juice of 1 lemon (better yet, lime)

1 bottle (great) tequila

1 tablespoon of *piloncillo* (Mexican dark sugar, but not
      necessary. Regular sugar is fine. If you like dry
      drinks, forget the sugar.)

Mix ingredients in a large bottle and let rest in darkness for at
least a month. Filter and drink *very* cold.

It's amazing. Look at the sun through your glass and you'll
think you are drinking liquid ruby.

Monsieur Diaz is dead now. The last time I saw him, he gave me
his gold spoon from *la vieille Russie,* and advised me to do something
"really frivolous" with whatever I could get for it, perhaps to exorcise
the austere role it had played in his life for so long.

I bought a very expensive bottle of scotch (which was stupid, because the hangover is the same with cheap booze) and a leather jacket
at Yves Saint Laurent.

Symbolically, 1492, the year of the discovery of the West Indies by Columbus, could be considered the year the last Crusade began. This one was supposed to bring the dawn of a new world. Catholic Europe—Spain, more precisely—was trying to spread the word of Christ over the whole world. Mostly by trying to reach unknown lands that many considered fantastical. Accounts of gold and precious-gem mines to be found there undoubtedly stimulated this passion for evangelism.

This crusade was sudden, brutal. It involved the rape of civilizations, of a whole humanity, one of the first historically documented genocides perpetuated in the name of the Gospel. Think of the traditional image of Saint Columbus bowing and kissing the very Catholic hand of Queen Isabel. How disgusting! It shows the same process of mythification that Che Guevara would be graced with five hundred years later. The murderer-on-commission turned martyr. Or sex symbol, which is, as far as mental comfort is concerned, nearly the same. As a child in the late seventies in Europe, I learned at school that Columbus was a hero who had "given us America." The price he—and the native Americans—paid was never mentioned.

The unknown lands Columbus opened up were full of promise. For the well-intentioned missionaries, they offered a second chance to build a church far away from Europe's excesses, a church that would at last incarnate the simplicity of Christ. But the white man's omnipotent arrogance had the last word. Considering themselves the only representatives of the only true civilization and the only true God, the priests tried ardently to fulfill their mission of saving the natives from eternal damnation, a concept, of course, entirely foreign to them.

Pope Alexander VI had called the era "the eleventh hour of humanity: A new way, and a new world to be conquered by the Gospel." This eleventh hour of humanity, brilliant with promise, would end in an orgy of butchery, spiritual and cultural. The conquerors brought with them their idea of Christian Empire, which meant for the native peoples submitting to the yoke of the Pope and the Spanish Empire. Along with Bibles, they carried new viruses that killed the natives, whose immune systems weren't prepared for smallpox. They rebaptized places and cities that had been known by other names for millennia. They brutally imposed a new god, determined to have him worshipped no matter what the price.

I have written this to make clear just why Juan Diego might have been confused by the requests of the "thing" on the hill, and by her way of calling him "dignified."

The bishop told him, "I will calmly listen to you another time. I have to see it from the very beginning, the reason you have come, and your will and your wish."

A way—kind, perhaps, but final—to tell him, "Go and get lost."

Back at our hotel, the receptionist informs me that I received a call from Lanore L. I've never met Lanore; she is the friend of a friend and lives in San Francisco. She is Mexican, in her late twenties, and studies religion in a college in the Bay Area. She comes to Mexico City often. When our common friend, Rina, heard that I was working on a book on Guadalupe, she told me, "You must meet Lanore. Guadalupe is her biggest problem."

We exchanged letters, preferring writing to phone calls. There have been a lot of missed rendezvous between us. All I know of her, apart from her difficult-to-read, spidery handwriting, is that Lanore was raised in an L.A. barrio. Strange that after months of back-and-forth, both living on the West Coast, we had to get together in the city of the apparitions.

We fix a time and a place to meet, not very far from the hotel, in Calle Londres near the "twin museums": a Ripley's Believe It or Not and the Museo de Cera, a wax museum. When I arrive, she is already there in the Ripley's parking lot leaning against a Porsche "identical to James Dean's." She wears a short, bright-green dress. She is cute, very small and skinny, with high cheekbones, more Maya than Aztec, rum-colored skin, and dark-brown, brilliant, slightly slanted eyes. She looks more like a girl-shaped clay vase than a real girl. She is warm and friendly and hugs me impulsively, gushing, "You are the only man that has written to me so much." She shows me two tickets. "The Ripley is the same here as in Helsinki: the mummified cat, the Jivaro shrunken head, the handcuffs of Houdini. I know that Houdini collected handcuffs, but still . . . he couldn't have had so many pairs. It's suspicious."

I reassure her and tell her that it's the same in France with Napoleon's deathbed. Each provincial museum owns a bedroom set upon which the emperor is supposed to have died; each set is, of course, authenticated by a vague descendant.

Lanore says, "I thought that the best place to talk would be the wax museum. There's never anybody there, and since you are writing on the ultimate Mexican myth, it's better to meet all of them at once."

We climb the staircase with its worn red carpet that could be in a well-kept French bourgeois home. The mansion where the museum is located is very Napoleon III/South American, in the flamboyant style common to some areas of Mexico City and Buenos Aires.

Lanore laughs. "These houses were built during the Maximilian and Carlotta era. Back then, it was indispensable to look European. Nowadays, you need to look and sound American. From my hotel to here, I counted three KFCs. It's more than you could find in the same distance in San Francisco." I tell her that one day, after a two-hour walk through a south Indian jungle, Andrew and I found, on the shore of a cobra-infested lake, a bamboo shack where a painted Stallone advertised the Rambo Bar.

We come to the first floor of the museum, an immense room with high mirrored walls and wax dummies whose identity, thank God, is mentioned on what looks like embossed business cards pinned to their costumes. They are all in a rigid straight line without any attempt at dramatic arrangement or plausibility, like the clay Chinese warriors in the Ming emperor's mausoleum. William Jefferson Clinton smiles inanely next to Mao (probably forgotten here; his hands are peeling and some fingers are missing). The Pope (who looks like Lloyd Bridges in papal regalia) seems to be sharing a great joke with the Dalai Lama. A dummy that I identify at first as Margaret Thatcher ends up being Elizabeth II.

In the next room is grouped the Mexican pantheon. Above everybody, a flamingly sensual Guadalupe stands on a resin rock, not at all pregnant and very curvy, with a glittering garish green coat and cinnabar-red lips; very Vegas–Tepeyac. She looks like an Italian movie star of the fifties.

Lanore is amused with my reaction. "Yes," she says, as if she had read my mind, "It's Gina Lollobrigida in the role of the Ever Virgin Mary." Still, her hands are joined in a prayer and her heavily made up eyes seem to be asking the grace of the ones around her; Emiliano Zapata, Plácido Domingo (with the sheet music of "Granada" in his hand), Dolores Del Rio (in black, severe as a saint) and—God knows why—John Wayne.

"You see," says Lanore, pointing at Lollobrigida–Guadalupe, "La Virgen belongs in the most extreme way in the popular iconography. She is our most famous movie star."

She walks on and stops near the wax visitor reading his paper, indispensable feature of all wax museums in the world. "I was told that they were forced to sew shut the zipper on Clinton's pants," she says in a serious voice. "People would make dirty jokes." She gives a long glance at the wax visitor and, ignoring the sign that says it's forbidden, sits next to him.

"Okay, come on," she says. "Ask me why I can't stand Guadalupe." At that moment, an androgynous skinny boy appears and starts to talk very fast, in a high voice. I don't understand a single word, and Lanore gets rid of him. "He sells pictures by computer. You know the type, your own face on the cover of *Vanity Fair*."

Suddenly, without my prompting, she talks openly. "I was born here; not very far from here, actually. My parents left for the States when I was four years old with my grandmother; they were grape pickers near Delano, in California. When I was growing up, there she was, La Virgen, on the wall, the Sagrado Corazón, San Martín de Porres, San Lázaro, but mostly La Madre, La Morenita. She was everywhere, like a reproach."

"And like the music of Vikki Carr," I add, echoing the conversations I have had with Chicanos born in the sixties.

"We didn't have money for music," Lanore says dryly. "We would go to my *tia*'s, across the street, to listen to ranchero music."

"What's ranchero music?"

"All Mexico is into ranchero music. It's sentimental, filled with '*mi corazón.*' Always the same story, the man that got away, a lot of trumpets, crying. Here it's called *ranchera, música ranchera.* I listen to it every day."

I tell her that I've been a fan of ranchero music for a long time without knowing it.

"My mother was beaten by my father, as her mother had been by my grandfather, and my father tells me, 'Maria, when she doesn't get it, she misses it.' When I was a teenager I told my mother to leave. She showed me La Virgen on the wall and said, 'She went through it all, why not me?' "

My first thought is that Lanore is exaggerating. First of all, Joseph has never been known as a wife abuser. Second, why universalize a problem based on a single remark?

Always a mind reader, Lanore looks piercingly at me and adds, "It was every woman's fate, still is. La Madre went through it all, why not us? It's good to suffer. You know, 'happiness is not for this world' and all that crap. In Mexican families, the man is the master, the wife cooks and bears kids, raises them, gets fat, and dies, and she needs to accept also the man when he wants it. That's how my mother talked about sex. The only time she ever mentioned it to me, she used the word 'accept.'" Lanore sweeps her forehead with a Kleenex. "It's hot here; not good with all that wax. Too bad you can't smoke here. . . ."

I try to joke to ease her mood. "Let's try and sit totally still and see if people squeeze us." It's lame and it doesn't work. Lanore glares at me and goes on.

"When I was thirteen, my mother told me, 'No Tampax. Only when you are married, *if* your husband allows it.' And this was in 1980!"

To reassure her I let her know that as a boy in the late seventies, I was convinced, mostly by my aunt, who was never good at talking about the birds and the bees, that babies were being delivered every Sunday by plane at the Roissy airport, then driven to the families who had placed orders.

Lanore doesn't hear me; she's too engrossed in her own story. "At seventeen, I went to see a gynecologist. Afterward, I told my grandmother. You know what she did? She shouted, 'If you have a problem, talk to me, to *tia,* to your mother. Don't pay to be molested!'" Suddenly Lanore's rage angers me. Abruptly, I say, "Yes, but what has Guadalupe to do with all that?"

She looks at me like a pediatrician at an autistic child. "We girls were supposed to imitate La Virgen in every part of our lives. Good! But why weren't the boys expected to be Christlike, then? Wouldn't that have been logical? *We* were punished for having bodies. Not them—they could have fun, have sex, have girlfriends, go to see the *putas.* Boys who had sex out of wedlock were sons of a gun; girls were whores. Guadalupe keeps her eyes down; so do the Mexican women. She accepts, so they accept." She slaps her thighs, a surprising gesture from someone otherwise so delicate. Perhaps she does so to look emancipated.

Lanore stands up abruptly and points to the stairs that lead down to the chamber of horrors. "Let's go down," she says, "into the kingdom of darkness." She smiles. I follow her down the winding rickety stairs. In the basement is a succession of small rooms with low ceilings, plunged in almost total darkness. All the monsters of the movies are there: Dracula, Frankenstein's creature, the werewolf, the mummy. In the next room Jeffrey Dahmer, hands covered with plastic blood, kneels in front of his open fridge with the disappointed look of one who's just found out there's no more Häagen-Dazs. A young couple walks in front of us. I hear them laughing without seeing them. The man is trying to scare the woman, who seems to enjoy it.

"These are happy, at least," I say to Lanore. She doesn't reply. Then she stops in front of a skeleton dressed in a monk's outfit. "Go to the cathedral, near the Templo Mayor; it's just the same there as here, horror everywhere . . . the difference is that there you don't pay an entrance fee."

"I've been to the cathedral several times, but it's always in restoration."

"It's always being restored," Lanore laughs. "Anyhow, it's just like here. Same wax bodies being tortured, burning in hell, pierced by arrows, beheaded, licked by flames. What does all that agony tell you but 'Suffer in silence'? It's through messages like that they've kept the poor, poor—here and everywhere else. At least in India they are honest. They adore the caste system. Here it's the Church that's in charge of the dictatorship."

I tell her that sometimes I think that the total acceptance of God's will is like the reaction of an abused child who endures everything while continuing to love his monster parents. "It's a question of perspective, I suppose," I add, suddenly at a loss.

She pauses and lights a cigarette.

"Last December, my mother was diagnosed with colon cancer. All night, I prayed at the feet of Guadalupe. All night, I tell you. It was the electric neon Lupe of my childhood. The crown is like a Christmas garland. If you turned the key, she sang a *mañanita,* but my brothers broke it long ago. All night I asked the Virgin to save my mother. You know what? My mother is fine."

Lanore smiles, her eyes suddenly brimming with tears. "That might be the first step toward reconciliation. There's a name for it, you know, like the people who go to see a shrink because they want a divorce." She laughs, visibly ashamed to be caught off guard.

"Someday, I hope that someone will find that the Tilma is a painting, that the Aztecs knew how to do it, that it was a kind of bad dream. Then I would be finally rid of Her altogether."

When he arrives at Tepeyac, Juan Diego finds the Lady of Light at the top of the hill. Embarrassed and ashamed of not having fulfilled his mission, he prostrates himself in the dust. "My owner, my matron, my Lady, the most abandoned of my daughters, my child, I went where you sent me to deliver your thought and your word. With great difficulty, I entered the place of the lord of priests; I saw him; before him, I expressed your words just as you had ordered me. He received me and listened carefully. But I know he did not believe me. He told me, 'You have to come another time. I will calmly listen to you another time.' I saw in the way he answered me that he thinks that possibly I am just making it up that you want a temple on this site, and possibly it is not your command. I beg you, my owner, my queen, my child, that you charge one of the more valuable nobles to come and take your message and your word, so it may be believed. Because I am just a piece of rope, a small ladder, the excrement of people; I am a leaf; they order me around, lead me by force; and you, my most abandoned daughter, my child, my lady and my Queen, send me to a place where I do not belong. Forgive me to cause pain to your heart, my Lady and my owner."

The Virgin answers him: "Listen, my most abandoned son, know well in your heart that there are not a few of my servants and messengers to whom I could give the mandate of taking my thoughts and my word and so that my will may be accomplished. But it is absolutely necessary that you personally go and speak about this, and that, through your mediation and help, my wish and my desire be realized. I beg you very much, my most abandoned son, and with all my energy I command that precisely tomorrow, you go again to see the bishop. In my name, you will make him listen well to my wish so that he may make my wish a reality and build a temple. And tell him once again that I personally, the Ever-Virgin Mary, the Mother of the God Teotl, I am the one who is sending you there."

Seeing how insistent she is, Juan Diego replies, "I will go there, and I will tell him truthfully your thought and your word. In no way whatsoever will I fail to do it; it will not be painful for me to go. I will go to do your will. But it could well be that I will not be listened to and not be believed. Tomorrow, when the sun sets, I will return your thought and word to you, what the bishop answered me.

"Now, I take leave of you, my most abandoned daughter, my child, my matron, now, you rest a bit."

And he goes back home. It has been quite a day.

The next morning at dawn, Juan Diego leaves his house once again to attend mass. After the service, once again, trying to fulfill his promise, he runs to the bishop's palace. And once again, he waits for hours. Juan Diego must be extremely upset. Put yourself in his place: You have a poor, uneventful life, and suddenly a floating, shining lady appears to you and asks you to convince the most important man in town that she wants a chapel built in the middle of nowhere.

The day after my meeting with Lanore, we decide to visit the house-museum of Frida Kahlo, in the plush suburb of Coyoacán.

The hotel receptionist whom we ask for directions tells us, as he does every time we want to go somewhere, "You don't want to go there," with a tone half interrogatory and half dismissive. As if he were psychic, he "knows" where we want to go and not go. We don't want to go to the pyramids by bus, to the flower market on Sunday, to the cemetery at noon, to the outdoor movie theater, and so on.

I have never really felt attracted by Kahlo's work. The avalanche of products with her effigy—calendars, paperweights, ashtrays, even Guadalupes with Kahlo's face (I've seen one in a store in Haight-Ashbury next to another one with Elvis's face)—disturbs me, like ties featuring van Gogh sunflowers or Munch's scream. However, since we are in Mexico City . . .

The green cab drives through neighborhoods we've never seen before. It's only nine in the morning, and the traffic jam is already hallucinatory. Maybe it's just the thought that we are leaving the downtown area, but I feel the air lighter, less smoggy. Well, it's all relative; there still are the fumes, mixed with the hot smell of cedar sap. Groups of chattering and giggling little girls are on their way to school. They wear uniforms: navy blue skirts and white blouses, some with red sweaters despite the heat. The oldest ones are made up like flamenco dancers and smoke Marlboros. Precocious Lolitas with stiletto heels and white socks, a dirty-old-man's heaven.

All at once, on the right, we see a huge cemetery. At the gates, there are several stands with flower arrangements, most of them made out of red carnations and gladiolas. I see one, white, guitar-shaped, certainly a special order. The driver tells us the names of the famous buried there. I don't know most of them. Our driver is short and gray-haired, the oldest one we've met so far. He points his finger toward a white column and says, "Lupe Velez." Andrew asks me who Lupe Velez was. The driver repeats her name, as if Lupe herself were crossing the street as he speaks. Lupe Velez was an exotic sensation, a beauty who made a lot of films. Like Carmen Miranda, she ended crushed by Hollywood's lack of care for pampas flowers. She was married for a while to Johnny "Tarzan" Weissmuller. In the end, like Carmen Miranda too, she took her own life. The driver listens to me; we are stopped in the traffic; he is old enough to have known Lupe Velez. With his two hands, he sketches in the air an hourglass figure, then hammers his chest with the scream of the jungle's son; we understand each other.

Frida Kahlo's street, in a residential area, is extremely calm. Number 247, where she lived, looks like a small fortress, with hyacinth-blue and coral-red walls.

At the gate, a guard, a stocky little tough guy, stops me and grabs my bag. "No photo," he barks, then gestures toward a small window where, we read, we can buy *"boletos para visitantes."*

We enter a large square flowerless garden with a lot of gigantic rubber plants, succulents, and thick-layered carpets of ivy on the ground. I return to ask the guard if the dominance of green succulents was Kahlo's wish. But he is playing a guard from Buckingham Palace now, and all I get is a stone face: It may be his only way to admit that he doesn't know.

In the concrete walls that surround the garden are embedded enormous shells—Kahlo thought that they were "vagina pink"—and dozens of Aztec idols. Perhaps they are originals after all; the interest in antiques is relatively recent in some parts of the world.

This color-drained vision of concrete and stark green creates a total contrast with the violent colors of outside. It's as if we have entered a pagan shrine.

Frida Kahlo was born in 1907 to a relatively wealthy family. Carlos Fuentes once wrote that "she had been murdered by life." She got polio at six or seven; at eighteen, the bus she was riding hurtled into a wall, and she was crippled for life. During her convalescence, she started to paint. At twenty-two, she married the painter Diego Rivera, who was considered—and considered himself—a national hero. They formed a strange couple, the crippled princess and the genial polymorphously perverse toad, linked by their leftist political passions (even though their communism was more left-wing caviar than the real thing) and united by a strange *amour fou*. Fuentes describes Frida's life: "She is hung naked from her feet, to strengthen her spinal column; she loses her fetuses in pools of blood; she is forever surrounded by clots, chloroform, bandages, and needles." Kahlo's life could be seen as a bizarre, tragic, bloody operetta, replete with colors, bodily secretions, and eroticism. She wrote of herself: "She stinks like a dead dog."

To hide her broken body, Kahlo used rich fabrics, ribbons, silk flowers. She decorated her hair with pearls and gardenias, and compared the women who tried to emulate her to "cabbages." Her work, however, is haunted by the broken feminine, as in The Broken Column, where she paints herself as a female Saint Sebastian. Everywhere in her drawings and paintings there are astounding images of the enslaved and violated feminine, echoing strangely what Lanore was trying to tell me yesterday, as if she were also somewhere looking for a feminine god to cry to and heal with or to share her pain.

Despite her health, Kahlo explored her sexuality and her bisexuality. She divorced Rivera, then married him again, and lived in the large Coyoacán house, treated like a kept mistress, when she was, in fact, his legitimate wife. She died in 1954, mythical in Mexico, but as yet unknown in the wider world. One year before, she had had her first one-woman show in a Mexico City gallery. In the same month—August 1953—her leg was amputated. Officially, Frida was said to have died of pulmonary complications. Her friends believed she committed suicide.

We are walking in Kahlo's queendom. Despite the intense heat outside, the house is cool, thanks to the thick walls, no doubt. Kahlo's faded dresses hang in glass cases like romantic suicides. Costume museums, especially those of famous people, are always like seeing someone in his coffin. Something has left, the something that once brought life to the fabrics. All that remains are the envelopes.

The kitchen is huge and yellow. There are paper sunflowers on a large table, too new to have known Kahlo's meals. There are some copies of her work framed with wooden roses; the originals are in the Dolores Olmedo Patiño Museum. Dolores Olmedo is the Mexican Peggy Guggenheim, still alive, and old as Lilith; she was Rivera's benefactor and loathed Kahlo.

To get to Kahlo's workshop, you have to take a dark staircase whose walls are smothered with old *retablos*. Rivera collected these naive ex-votos obsessively and traveled all around the country to find them. Some are painted on the backs of cigar cases, some on strips of steel. All thank La Lupe for protecting a baby from death, saving a mother from the suffering of delivery, bringing a new tractor to the farm, averting a deadly avalanche or lava flow.

Kahlo's atelier is a clear, sharp-angled room with bookshelves. On a tripod stands an unfinished portrait of Stalin, with her wheelchair nearby. In a corner, there's Kahlo's narrow bed, where she died on July 13, 1954. On the almost surreally delicate white lace blanket stretches her body cast. Like children who paint the plaster that protects a broken arm, Kahlo decorated her cast with birds and flowers, stars and garlands. The museum management has had the macabre idea to fix a light bulb inside. The beautiful guardian, an art history student with long, curly auburn hair and flashing, rich green eyes, who speaks a very Oxford-like English, turns it on in exchange for a story "about America." A lifetime's agony transformed into a work of camp art. The exorcism is complete.

On Kahlo's bedside, a big doll in peasant costume sits with perpetually staring purple eyes, and around the bed, piles of books are stashed: *El Loco,* by Kahlil Gibran; *Food for Gourmets; Talleyrand,* by Duff Cooper; the Viking Portable Library *Whitman; Memorias,* by Pancho Villa; *Le Temps Retrouvé,* by Proust; Elie Faure's *History of Art;* and *War and Peace.* On her bedside table someone has arranged *Toi et Moi* of Paul Géraldy, perhaps the cheesiest poems in French literature, so overhoneyed they seemed already out of fashion at the time of their publication in the thirties. Could she really have liked these?

Facing the bed, portraits of Marx, Stalin, Mao. No wonder Kahlo complained of insomnia!

Kahlo had an affair with Trotsky, yet cultivated Clare Boothe Luce as a friendly patron; she would read *Toi et Moi*, but enjoyed going to *palenques* to see cockfights, whose losers often end beheaded by the winners. Kahlo wrote in her diaries, "I would not wish to harbor any hope; everything moves to the beat of what's enclosed in the belly," while living in a pink-and-yellow house with paper flowers and wax fruits, a monstrous doll's house.

Was Frida Kahlo looking for some reconciliation between her tortured femininity and God? Or am I still too drenched by Lanore's depression? Perhaps Kahlo was simply a very harried, furious woman. She doesn't seem to have had any mystical crises ever, not documented ones, anyway. But her work. . . . One painting haunts me: A dark woman with breasts loaded with cancers feeds a horribly precocious baby Frida. What tragic wisdom is she filling her with? All the pictures of that brilliant woman, submissive to Rivera, nearly transparent, are those of a broken fairy in love with a toad that will never turn into a prince. Even if her art and lifestyle put her above the usual conditions of Mexican women, is there a parallel between her life and what Lanore was telling me yesterday? Did she bury herself alive for her man's sake? Is her art a constant cry for the liberation of a shattered woman from a male prison camp? And what would have happened to her or her work had she allowed her darkened heart to open to the Virgin on the old *retablos*?

On our way out, while I retrieve my camera, the girl at the souvenir shop asks us why we have come to Mexico City. It seems bizarre to the natives of this crumbling madhouse of a capital that anybody would choose to come here rather than go to Puerto Vallarta or Acapulco. I explain my choice, and at the name of Guadalupe, as always in Mexico, the three other people in the shop cross themselves, even the little tough guy.

The *Nican Mopohua* mentions that "he broke into tears when the prelate walked in." Another ordeal is coming. Zumárraga makes it clear that he is skeptical, to say the least, and that to even begin to consider Juan Diego's miraculous story as fact, he needs a sign. Nobody can blame him for asking this. Juan Diego tells him that he will ask the Lady if she will oblige; what else can he do?

He leaves the palace. The bishop then orders some of his guards to follow Juan Diego from a distance, to check with whom he talks, what he does, where he goes.

They lose him on the road to Tepeyac. He suddenly disappears from sight and is nowhere to be found. Feeling stupid, the bishop's men go back and report the strange fact to their master. At this point, they are all convinced that Juan Diego is a small-time crook, a tramp at best, or crazy. They will be much more persuasive with him if he ever comes back.

The next morning, Juan Diego is forced to face the fact that his uncle, Juan Bernardino, is doing really badly; actually, he is dying. The *Nican Mopohua* isn't precise about the nature of his illness, but it is an infectious fever, probably smallpox. The recently imported virus from the Old World kills the natives like flies. After a brief examination, the doctor tells Juan Diego that his uncle doesn't need him, but only the last rites.

Later that night, Juan Bernardino feels death approaching and begs his nephew to go out and find a priest. As he runs through Tepeyac Hill's rocky paths, Juan Diego decides that if he takes his usual route, the Lady will try to stop him and begin all over again her litany of requests. That, right now, is the last thing he needs. She will understand: His priority is the salvation of his uncle's immortal soul. So Juan Diego chooses another road. "He thought that having taken this other route, he would not be seen by the one who cares for everyone," says the *Nican Mopohua*. Never underestimate heaven.

From the other side of the hill, he sees her coming down from the top. She has been waiting for him: "My most abandoned child, where are you going, in what direction are you going?"

Too bad; he is caught. "My child, my most abandoned daughter, I hope you are happy, does your body feel all right, my owner and my child? You must know that my uncle, a poor servant of yours, is in his final agony. A great illness has fallen upon him, and he will die soon; I am going to your house to call a priest, so that he may go and hear confession and prepare him. After doing this, I will quickly return here. I will come back and fulfill the mission you gave me. Have patience with me, my matron and my child. I do not want to deceive you. Tomorrow, I will come quickly."

The Virgin replies, "Listen, and hear well in your heart, my most abandoned son, that which scares you and troubles you is nothing; do not let your countenance and heart be troubled. Do not fear that sickness or any other sickness or anxiety. Am I not here, your mother? Are you not under my shadow and my protection? Am I not your source of life? Are you not in the hollow of my mantle where I cross my arms? What else do you need? Is there anything else you need? Let nothing trouble you or cause you sorrow. Do not worry because of your uncle's sickness. He will not die of his present sickness. Be assured in your heart that he is already healed."

Then the lady points to the top of the hill, where she stood a few minutes before. "Go up, my most abandoned son, to the top of the hill, and there you will see many different flowers. Cut them, gather them, put them together. Then come down and bring them before me."

Back to La Villa, the new basilica, nine in the morning. Near the exit is the official souvenir store, just behind where the Tilma is displayed. It's a large octagonal room. Since the only other access to the outside, the monumental entrance doors, is far away, the only way to leave is to go through the store—"a good marketing strategy," as Andrew points out.

Exactly the same bazaar reigns here as outside, only here it is stamped with the approval of the basilica. Everything's slightly more expensive. A large poster, bigger, actually, than the real thing, and glued on canvas to look more "maguey," bears a note, written in gilded italics, that it is the only authorized representation of the Tilma. Despite the thousands of unauthorized images for sale outside, the trick seems to work. The official stamp is a good agent of conviction for the imploring soul: If it's approved by the bishop, the logic must go, it's even more likely to be approved by God, and so grace will come faster. If you buy something coming from the basilica, you're more likely to be granted your prayer. Poor people seem to be more susceptible to this blackmail than mean tourists like us, who buy cheap outside. The clergy must be making a tidy fortune on this obvious racket, while discouraging the populace from "exaggerated cults and superstition." Another masterpiece of Catholic hypocrisy.

In front of us a withered, slightly stooping Indian woman with a silver-white braid in the shape of a scorpion's tail is buying a large, framed, authorized Tilma. The way you pay is strange here. You show a shop girl the item you want to purchase, she gives you a receipt that you bring to the other side of the room. There, behind gigantic mirrors, agitated hands grab your money and give you back a stamped paid receipt. Then, slightly dazed already, you join a long line (business is good) and exchange your piece of paper for your relic. The women working there are charmless: bulldog-stinking old nuns and younger, mute, tough girls made up à l'américaine. Don't even try to smile or thank them, it won't work. They will only make you feel awkward, as if you had just tried to make a pass at them. Clerks hand you over your purchases with the febrile speed of people buying girlie magazines in airport stores.

I am fascinated by the real usefulness of the mirrors. They are not bulletproof (I've asked); they are no more protective than bathroom mirrors. Their only function is something more hypocritical, a gesture toward shame at making money in this holy place. The woman with the braid like a scorpion's tail takes her turn before me. She is very upset because the two hands behind the mirrors are telling her that she is six pesos (not even a dollar) short. The nun, who, so far, has behaved in a very aloof, nunlike fashion, barks at her because she wrapped the image for nothing. The little woman is close to tears. I give her some change: She accepts it eagerly, promising me and my family all the blessings of the One who reigns here. The nun, suddenly serene again, vaguely checks if the wrapping's all right. The old woman walks back to the mirrors to pay, a triumphant smile on her face. Triumph can't be a feeling she experiences every day.

The man behind me in line, an old German tourist, notes what is going on. He tells me sadly, "Pilgrimages are okay for tourists, but if you are a believer, I have always thought it was harder to believe here."

"Yes," I answer, "and all of this goes on fifteen yards from the Tilma."

The nun, who must think I am rich, hands me an image of Guadalupe.

"Take it," says the German. "It's free, after all. Here, it could be a sign that grace is already working for you. You know what they say: 'Poor Mexico, so close to the USA, so far from God.' "

Then, very upset, he repeats the words I used, "And all of this fifteen yards from the Tilma. And in Lourdes, or all around the world, it's the same thing. At Lourdes, they bark at people in wheelchairs fifteen yards from the rock where Bernadette knelt. I travel all year long to holy places and sometimes I think I'm an idiot: There's nothing like your own home to reach out to God from." We stand together silently. Then he says, "But if I had stayed at home I wouldn't have seen her, would I?"

Juan Diego climbs the hill, very skeptical. How can he be otherwise? The soil of the hill is extremely poor all year long; he has never seen any flower there, and it is December, the heart of winter!

The top of the hill is covered with flowers, precious little blossoms called Castilian roses, which look like wild eglantine. It is the flowering earth! The hill is covered with all kinds of flowers from Castile, full of dew and shining brilliantly, although it is the time when ice hardens upon the earth.

The roses, moreover, are very fragrant. Juan Diego starts to cut them and place them in the hollow of his mantle. Then he takes them down to the Queen of Heaven. When she sees the flowers, she takes them one by one into her small hands and then replaces them in the hollow of his mantle. The mantle he wears, like that of everybody else of his class, is a piece of woven cactus fiber called a *tilma*.

"My most abandoned son, these flowers are the sign that you will take to the bishop. In my name, tell him that he is to see in them what I want, and with this, he should carry out my wish and my will. You are my ambassador; in you I place all my trust. With all my energy, I ask you that *only* in the presence of the bishop are you to open your mantle and let him know and reveal to him what you are carrying. You will recount everything well. You will tell him how I sent you to climb to the top of the hill to go cut the flowers, and all that you saw and admired.

With this you will change the heart of the lord of the priests so that he will do his part to build and erect my temple."

Juan Diego, holding wrapped in his *tilma* the proof of his celestial encounters, runs once again to the bishop's mansion.

He is in for a rough reception. The guards who recognize him tell him to go away, call him a liar and a fool, and tell him he will never get to bother His Eminence ever again; enough is enough.

As he has done before, Juan Diego sits and waits. The fact that he holds his *tilma* rolled up in an overprotective way is intriguing to the guards. A *tilma* is meant to be worn on the shoulders, not carried as a relic, especially on such a cold morning. The guards insist on seeing what is in it. Juan Diego refuses. At one moment, feeling especially threatened, he lets a few petals fall on the floor to prove to them he isn't the liar they say he is. The bishop's people are astonished. Castilian roses in December? Now that is a miracle! Or witchcraft. Three times, the guards try to grab the *tilma,* and three times Juan Diego escapes from them. By then completely mystified, they give in to his request to see the bishop, mostly to see what is in the *tilma.*

Juan Diego throws himself at the feet of the lord of the priests.

"My owner and my lord, I have accomplished what you asked for. I went to tell my matron, my owner, the Lady from heaven, Holy Mary, that you had asked a sign in order to believe me, so that you might build a temple where she is asking you to erect it. And besides, I told her that I had given you my word that I would bring you a sign and proof of her will. And today, when it was still night, she sent me to come and see you once again. And she agreed to give me the sign you asked for."

Juan Diego opens his *tilma* to show the bishop and his entourage the harvest of flowers. The roses fall to the floor. At the same time, on the *tilma*'s thick, vulgar fabric, cheap and scratchy as a coconut door-mat, is printed the exact image of the Lady from Tepeyac, "the precious image of Holy Mary, Mother of the god Teotl, the very image that would be worshipped to this day as *Reina de México y de las Américas, Nuestra Señora de Guadalupe*."

The controversy about the apparitions of Tepeyac began almost immediately. News of them spread like wildfire. Hundreds of thousands of Aztecs, believing that their Tonantzin had returned, converted to the new religion. Father Toribo's "Indian History" estimates that, in the ten years following the events, some nine million Indians became Catholics.

The transfer of La Tilma from the bishop's palace to the freshly built Ermita at the center of the city took place at the end of December 1531; the traditional date is the twenty-sixth. Whatever the date, one thing is certain: The shrine was built in record time.

The transfer of the relic provoked intense popular fervor. The shores of the lake of Texcoco were covered with boats filled with cut flowers. Thousands of people followed the church procession. Some became overenthusiastic and started to shoot arrows into the sky. One of them landed and pierced an Indian's chest, killing him instantly. His body was carried to the Tilma. Immediately he sprang to his feet, wondering how he had managed to get so close to the miraculous image, and went on celebrating. With this kind of Old Testament miracle, the conversion of a whole nation was guaranteed. Probably, also, the aspect of a miracle "too good to be true" aroused skepticism from the beginning and, understandably, about the whole affair.

Just before I left for Mexico, my friend Sonia called me.

"You *must* meet Dolores G." Like Sonia, Dolores is a million-airess, and collects art and famous people. I didn't see why I should meet her (being neither a Benin bronze nor famous).

"She'll *adore* you," Sonia gushed. Even though I enjoy being adored, I still didn't see why I should meet her or why she would adore me. However, not knowing if I will have my necessary quota of adoration in Mexico, I ring her.

Dolores also lives in Coyoacán. The cab takes the same route as last week when we went to see Frida Kahlo's house. Near the cemetery (where Lupe Velez's grave is) the driver stops suddenly. He's a very young man, skinny, with only a smattering of hairs on his face. Seeming deeply depressed, he tells me that he must call his wife. He points out a cafe to me and leaves with his Egon Schiele eyes and all the misery of the world bending down his shoulders.

I find myself sitting at a table across from the cemetery, nearly on the highway, with dust blowing across my hands and into my eyes. Just behind me, there's a small room painted in wild canary yellow with a cooler advertising ersatz Coca-Cola; next to me, a stand with different kinds of pretzels and cookies. The *número uno* brand of cookies in Mexico is called Bimbo.

An old man in fading, filthy khaki shorts walks by. He wants to sell me a water bottle with a belt so you can carry it around your neck or shoulder. He puts the bottle in my hand: Just look, he tells me. I give it back and he walks away, sad and hunched, loaded down with dozens of pink, blue, and yellow bottles. I should have bought it. I suddenly feel awful. It would have cost me just twenty cents, perhaps. But how could I arrive at Dolores G.'s with a pink plastic bottle in one hand? I felt disgusted with myself for worrying about appearances.

The old woman who sells cookies at the stand ends my self-flagellation by offering to read my palm. "Wonderful future," she says. She smiles encouragingly, displaying a row of dramatically blackened teeth. I think to myself, "If I stay any longer so close to the cars that sometimes graze my knee, my future lies across the street, in the *Panteón Dolores.*" I say no, but still feeling putrid about the old man, I buy my self-esteem back by giving the woman with the black teeth five dollars. She checks the bill in the light to see if it is not fake, then, reassured, offers me an aluminum medal of the Virgin of the Rue du Bac in Paris, where the Madonna appeared to Sister Catherine Laboure in 1830. I lived nearby for a while; I used to walk to the sanctuary every afternoon.

Now a little girl arrives, violently made up, and displays tapes on my table while the old woman reads the palm that she has grabbed by force. The tapes are pirates of Mariah Carey, *The Bee Gees Greatest Hits,* and several battered copies of another, which I buy: *Mañanitas por la Virgen de Guadalupe.* The skinny driver comes back and, without losing his melancholic gaze, offers to marry me to his sister, who is, he assures me, very beautiful, very fertile, and cooks like a goddess. Dolores's address and my dollars must have convinced him that I was Mr. Right or Mr. Green Card. André Breton's comment about visiting

Mexico crosses my mind: "There is no place for our movement here; surrealism is a way of life in this country."

After twenty more minutes in the traffic jam, trying to convince the driver that I wouldn't make such a good brother-in-law, we arrive at Dolores's mansion. It looks like a Mexican version of Tara in *Gone With the Wind,* with soaring white columns and two life-size Capodimonte panthers on each side of the front entrance. A short alley leads to a flight of white marble steps like those of an Arab tomb. From each side, from equally white marble walls, pour waves of plumbagos, heavenly blue like frozen cascades.

A tiny, thin butler with obviously dyed hair and mustache opens the door. His outfit is out of a Noël Coward play, and he looks disguised with a fixed smile. Saying nothing he walks me slowly through a white corridor to a large room opening to a pond covered with brilliantly colored water lilies—plastic ones, I soon realize.

The set is hallucinatory. It's like walking into the pages of *Architectural Digest* gone crazy. The walls are decorated with frescoes: fat-buttocked peasants carrying farm tools, red carnations, bouquets of calla lilies, no doubt by a bad but besotted student of Rivera. I know from Sonia that Dolores is a friend of the other Dolores—Dolores Olmedo, patron of Rivera and of any other Mexican painter or sculptor who flattered her. Sonia had said, "The two Doloreses are not close anymore. Don't ask me why."

All around me, all the furniture is white. Mae West's bathroom must have been something like this. A moldy polar bear skin sprawls in the center. The mantel of the tall fireplace is crowded with what look like conquistador helmets. Above it soars a superb Vuillard, the portrait of a radiant young woman holding lilac branches lit up by spring sunlight. Farther along on the same wall blares the portrait of La Señora, multiplied by four, by Andy Warhol, her red lips open like booby traps. Potted camellias line the four walls. The plants are real, but the flowers are fake, obviously glued onto the branches. Just looking at them makes me shudder a little.

Enter Señora Dolores from a door on the right of the fireplace. She's small and hunched; she wears an extraordinary dress with pale pink and white poppies that make her look like a mummified wedding cake. She must be at least eighty, with hair so black it's blue, and a heavily retouched face that is still—if bizarrely—beautiful, above the little shriveled body that barely counts anymore.

She shakes my hand firmly and tells me, "You are much too young to wear white. What will you wear at forty? Light colors are for older people." She touches her chin with the tips of two fingers. "The more it comes down here, the lighter colors you should wear." Then she sits abruptly and barks orders for tea. The disguised butler, to my surprise, replies in the same tone. Waiting for tea, Dolores obsessively arranges and rearranges the little objects on a low coffee table before her: an amethyst rosary, an ivory Buddha, a Russian lacquer box, a collection of old lead soldiers. A whisper, like the humming of wings, attracts my attention. I look around for a dragonfly and then realize that the dry murmur is coming from the Señora's gigantic eyelashes going slowly up and down.

She rubs the dust off an antique ink bottle, cursing, "The maids you can get these days! It was Empress Josephine's ink bottle," she goes on. "My friend Dolores Del Rio received it from some Hollywood people as a wedding gift. She married Cedric Gibbons, you know, very influential in the movies, but very vain and stupid. When she left him— not a moment too soon!—she came back to the country she never should have left."

Her voice is a bell-clear dark mezzo that doesn't hesitate on any word.

"It's a souvenir from my dear Dolores," she adds, as if I had asked. "I was *so* much younger than she. How, when did she die?"

Very fast, I realize that every object around her needs a prestigious past. The large red leather easy chair, she will soon tell me, is from Malmaison. (Even the leather seems to me very young to have supported the imperial behind.) The embroidered pillow on it with the motto "Love lasts forever" was embroidered by Martha Washington "during one of George's interminable absences." The mother-of-pearl fan on the coffee table once belonged to Maria Malibran, "the great singer," she adds, "who had the absurd misfortune of dying young after being flung from a horse." She lives surrounded by objects with pedigrees, imaginary or not.

The butler-in-disguise at last brings tea and fruit paste, set out on a large, circular silver dish like an Aztec calendar. Another dish bears *tamales dulces,* filled with hot cherry jam. I didn't know that tamales could be sweet, I tell her, and she gives me a look doubting my capacity to write a book about Mexico. Then she banishes the butler with an imperious gesture that makes the half-dozen bracelets on her wrist rustle together like an Indian rain stick.

"Why are you interested in La Virgen?" she asks, a little bored, as if to imply "when we could be talking about myself." When saying "La Virgen," she doesn't cross herself. That wouldn't fit her role at all.

Without waiting for an answer (so far I've said almost nothing), she sweeps into a Norma-Desmond-working-for-*National-Geographic* tirade. According to her, "Mexico doesn't exist anymore. America is destroying slowly the Mexican tradition, the Mexican culture.

"Two weeks ago, I was in my house in Puerto Vallarta . . . Do you know Puerto Vallarta? Oh, it was paradise on earth. Now, they have a statue of Liz Taylor with Richard Burton! Yes! Because of *The Night of the Iguana,* you know. And at their feet, they have an iguana! Imagine! All that beauty on earth, all God's wonder, and what? A resin statue of Liz Taylor!" She spits out "Liz Taylor" as if saying some unspeakably filthy swear word. Then she starts to cough and is soon choking in an alarming way. She clutches her chest and turns white, despite the thickness of her makeup. I imagine the story in the Mexican tabloids if she were to die now: *"Milionaria se muera con un joven—la última conversación es sobre Liz Taylor"* (Millionairess dies with a young man— her last conversation is about Liz Taylor).

The butler-in-disguise runs in with a glass of water, but she gets rid of him with the same theatrical and noisy gesture as before. Her tirade begins again: "The country is becoming the vision the Americans have of it." It's a phrase she must have said often because she seems proud of it.

"Even in the country—the deep, deep country?" I ask.

"Well, it's slower, still, when I was a young woman—when I was a child, in fact—the mariachis wore red peasant clothes. Beautiful peasant countrymen, that's what they were. And now! Look at now." She is vehement again; I check to see if there is water in sight. "Now they look like Hollywood mariachis with glitter on their hats and ridiculous costumes! And here are these imbeciles of Mexicans, dressed as their caricature!" She lights a cigarette; I am surprised she doesn't use a gold cigarette holder. She seems to appreciate the fact that I smoke with her. She smiles at me conspiratorially.

"The smoke, it disinfects the pipes. Never a cold, never!" She touches her faded cleavage. "Never any bronchitis either!" She pauses for a moment and then remembers her theme again. "Don't forget that in Argentina tango was a poor man's dance before Paris discovered it! You could see these big fat men dancing the tango with their gray suits, lifting one leg, like a dog peeing! What do you want from Mexico, the whole country's just an image from the past, and maybe a past that never existed."

"Or maybe existed long ago," I add, hoping to keep her angry and succeeding.

"Pooh!" she almost screams. "Think about *your* Europe and what the Americans think is European. They try so hard to look European, like in *your* Europe."

She insists on *your* Europe, as if I were paying a mortgage on it every month. She pours us tea, obviously thrilled with her lecture. Then she says, as abruptly as she does and says everything, "My grandfather had a passion for the Virgin of Guadalupe!"

Ah, here we come, she is going to talk about what I came for.

"You've heard about my grandfather, of course."

I shake my head. She starts a litany of names, places, nobility titles that I have never heard of. Then she arrives at the death-of-Grandpa episode; there, she enjoys silent pauses. The great *raconteuse* she is, she must have told this diamond of all her stories a million times. She announces, "This is an incredible story, even for me," and she claps her hands for another pot of tea, "immediately and hot."

She leans forward. "I have only Darjeeling. Tiny little monkeys pluck the leaves that go into it."

She flutters her hands with their endlessly long bright fuchsia nails as if she were speaking of butterflies and not of monkeys; and as if I had never seen tea fields.

Then she coughs, clears her throat, and begins. "My grandfather lived in an immense house—immense. *Era muy macho*—he was quite a man. When the revolutionaries of Pancho Villa were approaching, they (my grandfather, my mother, and the *jardinero*) decided to leave the hacienda. They wanted to go to the mountains to another house. So Grandfather left, dressed all in white (Knize would make all-white suits especially for him). He would wear them with a plumbago flower on his jacket. It's for him, all that plumbago here.

"In the forest, he sat against a tree, a fig tree, and he said to my mother, 'I'm dying, I am leaving,' and there he was, dead!" She clicks her fingers, and it sounds, indeed, like the soul leaving the body. "It was *soooooo* hot, they couldn't take him with them. My mother and the *jardinero* decided to bury him at the foot of the fig tree."

She pauses once again. I believe that her story is finished and I cannot see what is so extraordinary about it. But she continues, "Years later, once calm and peace settled, my uncle, my mother, a priest, and the *jardinero* returned to the forest to exhume Grandfather and take him to the family mausoleum. They were doing it clandestinely, you know. It was a time when everybody was killing everyone else, and when everybody was suspicious of everybody.

"Well, they arrived and started to dig at the bottom of the fig tree and they found Grandfather—his bones, anyhow. There were only bones left. And then they realized they had two skulls and more than two legs. Somebody else was buried with Grandfather! My uncle said, 'Papa and I had the same size hat.' He took off his sombrero and tried it on a skull, then on the other, but the skulls were nearly the same. Nobody knew which was Grandfather's or what to do. Eventually the priest said, 'These are two people here who need a Christian burial, so we'll take back both of them.' And that is what they did."

She drinks a sip of the monkey-harvested tea. I tell her that I think her grandfather was the more deeply buried skeleton and that someone else was buried on top of him. The earth had been dug up once, so it would be easy to dig up again.

She marvels, "What an interesting perspective! How, really . . . but now they are all mixed in the coffin. But the priest was adamant: Grandfather would need all of his bones on Judgment Day, every single one; otherwise, how could he be completely reassembled? They buried him for good during the night, in our mausoleum. There is an unknown man in the midst of our own. At least he is in good company."

Night is falling. I won't get a thing about Guadalupe except that her multiple grandfather "had a passion for her." "He wouldn't do a thing without asking her. Not a thing."

Dolores walks me out herself. At the door she says, "Wait, I have a present for you."

She comes back nearly immediately with a framed picture, her heavily retouched portrait, of course, an ageless Dolores in a golden setting sun. She must give a lot of portraits away.

I try my last chance, the *última,* to know something about La Virgen. Dolores was supposed to know so much about it, according to that damned Sonia. Dolores sticks her little triangular face between the two white doors, a carefully rehearsed effect. "You know, in the universities all around the world they've been studying how Pancho Villa could be so smart while being so uneducated. When they exhumed him three years after his death, they stole his head. They cut it off, in fact. Nobody knows where his head is. And the blood, three years later, was still fresh, and it ran and ran."

Mexico had been conquered ten years before, in 1521. The Aztecs were a proud people who, strangely, shared similarities with the Hebrews. Originally nomads, they became ambitious and grandiose builders, with elaborate ideas of caste that permitted them to oppress their own people without any scruple. They believed they were the chosen ones of God.

Then suddenly they were conquered and both spiritually and militarily shattered. They lost hope and gave up. At the time of the apparitions, the people around Tenochtitlán were plunged into the abject despair of a race deprived of its gods—depressed, alcoholic, raped. The Aztecs had believed in an astrological prediction whose date, "the Fifth Sun," matched the arrival of the Spaniards. They knew, in a confused way, that their time was over. Some scholars are convinced that is why they capitulated when they could have destroyed the Spanish armies so easily.

What could be done, in the circumstances, to alleviate tension? Such hatred could have been potentially explosive. Why not a good old miracle, something flashy and glittering, something supernatural that would impress these people, so superstitious already, so inclined to believe in messages from above? One brilliantly orchestrated miracle would release the pressure, like steam from a pot of boiling water.

For those who believe in the apparitions, Guadalupe arrived when the night was dark, when everything seemed lost. (The *Nican Mopohua* opens with the words: "It was still dark." In Aztec mythology, darkness is symbolic of cosmic birth.) For skeptics, the apparitions represent the shrewdest political adjustment an invader could devise. Naturally, the skeptics have had a field day, generating mountains of books, some widely researched, others written with such bad faith and vitriol that the popularity of document shredders can easily be understood.

In 1556, Francisco de Bustamante, a Franciscan from Toledo, wrote one of the first and most virulent attacks against the cult of Guadalupe. Probably because he disliked Alonzo de Montifar, successor of the late Zumárraga (who had died in 1548, two days after Juan Diego, both very old for their time), who had a very strong devotion to the Tilma. Also, it was an era in which Franciscans were influenced by Luther's writings and his hatred of images and statues.

Bustamante started by investigating the miracles and then began to question them. He made clear that one of the councils of Latran threatened to excommunicate anybody who busied himself with the "propagation of false miracles." Moreover, he insisted on the fact that the devotion to Guadalupe was, in fact, a barely disguised substitute for worshipping Tonantzin (missionaries would tear out their few remaining hairs trying to prevent Indians from adoring crosses with the idols of Aztec gods buried underneath them). Bustamante wrote that "church authorities" (i.e., Zumárraga and then Montifar) had encouraged a cult that could become very dangerous. Even more dramatically, he declared that the Tilma was the work of a painter and that he knew the man, an Indian artist and forger called Marcos (history has preserved only his first name). The most amusing line in Bustamante's sermon reads, "The image was regarded as miraculous in the sense that it worked miracles, not that it was miraculous in origin." Brilliant in its way.

Over the centuries, Bustamante's sermon has both aroused tremendous anger and engendered innumerable imitators. One of the most recent responses to it is *Our Lady of Guadalupe*, by Stafford Poole. This is a remarkable book, extraordinarily well documented and about as much fun to read as an IRS audit notice. Poole reverses five hundred years of devotion, with many historic sources, needless to say, very subjectively interpreted. He dismisses any evidence for the apparitions out of hand, while embracing the most fragile fact against them. Prudently, Poole stops his book just before the scientific discoveries about the Tilma that helped—or helped to help—the authentication of the image. The outside of the book does not indicate any of the controversy inside. Since it's published by the University of Arizona Press, can we see here a marketing strategy that would help sell the book in the Southwest, where "Guadalupos" are legion? Or was it the designer's choice?

On the other hand, let's be honest: The actors of the original drama do not help things. One of the biggest enigmas of Guadalupe is embarrassing, even for die-hard Guadalupos: the nearly total lack of documents written at the time of the apparitions. How to explain too the complete silence of Zumárraga about them? One of the reasons given for this—and one hard to swallow—is lack of paper. It is true, though, that Mexico didn't have much paper in those days. In a letter to Charles V, Zumárraga himself explains, "Little progress can be made with our printing through scarcity of paper; this is an obstacle preventing the publication of many works." Yet even if the letter is from the hand of the bishop, it is difficult to believe that no one would have found *some* paper to relate the amazing facts of Tepeyac. The only autograph we have from him that could be related to the Tepeyac files is an invitation asking the empress to appear at the Marian festivities of December 26, 1531. Nonbelievers, of course, will claim that this is just a mention of the Feast of the Immaculate Conception, and point out that there's no mention of the miracles.

So where do we stand? Zumárraga was a complex man and a great politician. I believe that his silence was purely political. He was caught between two fires: On one side, the Aztecs, always ready for a little war with someone; on the other, the Spanish authorities, who wouldn't have hesitated to condemn someone too interested in the natives' human rights. Evidently, Zumárraga, although the first man ever to contemplate the Tilma, was also a prudent Franciscan. What he did, almost certainly, was to encourage the cult with the natives while try-ing to keep it low-key as far as the Spanish authorities were concerned. This was his only way to keep his job and perhaps his head.

Visit to Teotihuacán, "the place where men become gods," according to the etymology. Other translators prefer "the place where gods are born."

Located twenty-five miles from the Mexico City, Teotihuacán is a complex of pyramids and buildings, most of them with religious purpose, connected to one another by a titanic Avenue of the Dead. Popular belief calls it the Aztec ruins, but the site was abandoned long before the Aztecs took possession of it. They gave back, for a while, its sacred identity by performing rituals there—often bloody ones—to cool down the mood swings of the sun god.

The buses that go to the pyramids leave from a station in the south of the city. Of course, the first driver takes us to the north station. He gets lost in a vegetable market, but that doesn't stop him from whistling and asking every forty seconds, "Teotihuacán, right?"

After a visit to each and every bus station in this part of Mexico City, we finally arrive at the right one. It looks like a long warehouse, surrounded by little rivers of mud and kids playing in the mud. Postcards and *gorditas;* a woman tries to sell me postcards of the pyramids. "Don't go, too hot! Just buy my cards. Better view than the real thing."

It's true that it's too hot. The heat makes everything vibrate and dance like the air above a flame.

In the waiting room inside the station, a young man is having his future read by "lucky birds." "Lucky" is a weird choice of word; the birds, often canaries, are sealed for life in cages where they can barely open their wings. The poor creatures pick rolled pieces of paper, similar to those you find in fortune cookies, and the message is supposedly an oracle from the *devas* of nature (as if they would associate with people locking birds in micro-cages). The young man is arguing with the bird master loudly enough to attract the attention of a policeman. (That tells you how loud it is.) In the line to climb onto the bus, I ask the man why he is so angry. "The bird told me that I was going to take a trip," he says, grimacing.

The bus is air-conditioned. As soon as it has left the suburbs of Mexico City, the driver stops and a singer-guitarist boards. For ten minutes he sings the classics of *ranchera* and all the melodies you can hear in a Mexican restaurant in Oslo or Casablanca: "Guantanamera," "Granada," "Perdóname." Just before he starts walking up and down to ask for tips, he sees how many American tourists there are and launches loudly into "My Heart Will Go On."

I have brought with me today the excellent *Ancient Mexico,* by Frederick Peterson. It was written in the late fifties, yet it's still one of the best books on the subject. Like many good books, it's out of print.

In 1959, visiting Teotihuacán, Peterson wrote:

> According to the legend, the gods lived in Teotihuacán, and the Sun and the Moon were created there . . . Teotihuacán began about 150 B.C., in the last stage of the preclassic culture. Its destruction was probably around 850 A.D. Excavations by Sigvald Linne on the outskirts of Teotihuacán show that the Toltecs moved in after it had been destroyed.

Teotihuacán was a "planned" city. It didn't just "grow." A group of priest-architects laid out the central city. Of course, it was not built all at once. There were obviously several additions to the original plan. The urban center was built around a long series of plazas and a long, wide, straight street formed the city's main axis. The present archeological zone covers almost seven square miles—the cooperation of the vast numbers of people involved in building the great metropolis must have required a stable and powerful society with strongly centralized authority. . . .

Few places in Mexico have been so intensively explored as Teotihuacán. Excavations began in 1889, but yet we know comparatively little of its cultural life and affiliations . . . many buildings are invisible to the casual viewer because they lie beneath the cornfields or are buried under the rubble dust and vegetations of centuries. . . . The valley around Teotihuacán was a cultural center, dominating a region over a hundred miles in all directions. . . . Three building phases can be discerned at Teotihuacán; at the end of the third phase, fire destroyed the greater part of the city and its culture shifted to the north of the actual Mexico City . . .

The pyramid of the Sun looked very different a millennium ago. Fifty years ago [circa 1909], when it could still have been restored, a pioneer archeologist, ironically called "Guardian of the Monuments," noticed the terrible state in which it had fallen. With the thought it could not be reconstructed in the time allowed, he decided to get down to the building underneath by "peeling like an onion." He made a slight miscalculation. There was no stone building inside. Under his direction, thousands of tons of stone were removed. The earthen masses inside were exposed to torrential rains and the pyramid began to dissolve . . . the entire pyramid was thrown out of symmetry, and a monstrosity resulted . . . the "Guardian of the Monuments" removed all remains of the covering, but left the anchor stones projecting from the central mass. What we see today is not the pyramid, but its core.

Some forty years have passed since Frederick Peterson explored Teotihuacán and wrote this. Even now, the access to the archeological site is a difficult one. There are several control posts where your identity and material are checked. It is virtually forbidden to film there unless you tip one of the guards, dressed as B-movie Che Guevaras. It is actually more difficult to get inside Teotihuacán than to go through Mexican customs (one of the easiest legal things I have ever done).

Just before you enter by the Temple of Quetzalcoatl (considered and called "the citadel" for centuries; it never was a citadel) and just before the long Avenue of the Dead, straggles a very lively little street of stores where you can find, all in the same shop, an Aztec obsidian whistle, a New York City map (circa 1989), and a Michael Jordan T-shirt (Jordan, surprisingly, doesn't seem to endorse anything Mexican so far). Drinks—even soft drinks—are forbidden inside Teotihuacán itself, for good reasons. Trying to buy a Pepsi there is like buying pot in the subway. The dealer feigns not to understand what you mean, then looks around and miraculously finds a bottle of soda that he sells you for the price of a soul.

When you face the Temple of Quetzalcoatl, the feathered-snake god, you take a left turn that opens onto a complete panorama of the city. On the right of the avenue stands the vast mass of the Sun Pyramid. At the end of the avenue rises the Pyramid of the Moon, a step pyramid, like those of Sakkara in Egypt. The Pyramid of the Moon is surrounded by smaller look-alike pyramids, grouped like little ducks around their mother.

Despite the chattering crowds, there is something morbid about the atmosphere. In the center of the avenue, endlessly criss-crossed by Aztec art dealers raising clouds of dull red dust, a group of men covered with feathers and beads, nearly naked (and not the kind you want to see naked), dances around a circle of seashells and oil lamps while one of them marks a hypnotic tempo, always the same, on his drum. All this looks like one of those films of Stewart Granger where he is either discovering emerald mines in deepest Africa or the ruins of Atlantis, and always delivering Debra Paget from hordes of unknown tribes dressed just like this. I think of Dolores G. and her tirade against Hollywood mariachis.

The Aztecs were convinced that they had to treat the sun as a capricious lover, and that the only way to deal with him was to give him an incessant avalanche of presents, human lives being his favorite. And since the presents, to be effective, had to be ultimately precious, it was the young and the beautiful they usually chose to sacrifice.

In 1978, construction workers digging near the Zócalo (the administrative and religious center of Mexico City) discovered one of the most exciting sites of modern archeology, the Templo Mayor (big temple). Until then, its existence and location had been questionable. Some had it located under the cathedral of the Zócalo (a clever way to prove Catholicism's supremacy over the bloodthirsty barbarians). Only the foundations of the temple are visible today. At the bottom of the big staircase, the workers exhumed a statue of the moon goddess, Coyolzauhaui. Human sacrifices were thrown down the stairs after their hearts had been torn out. The moon, it was believed, would welcome their disemboweled bodies.

The Templo Mayor itself is an offering. Immediately after the colonization of Tenochtitlán, around the fourteenth century, the Aztecs erected a thanksgiving monument whose final version is the Templo Mayor. It is estimated that twenty thousand people perished as sacrifices during the ceremonies of dedication.

One of the most revealing documents about this era is the Florentine Codex, written and illustrated by Friar Sahagún. It's kept in Florence, from where it derives its name. The illustrations of Indians sacrificing to their idols, or being massacred themselves, are hair-raising, but it is also filled with beautifully observed information about the daily life of the Aztecs. Its depictions of Aztec mothers pounding cornmeal or tending their gardens or dancing with their naked children are moving in their direct simplicity. The codex is, in fact, a giant cartoon illustrating a detailed story of Mexico just before and after the Spanish invasion, and a priceless revelation of the world to which Guadalupe appeared, in all its bloodiness and primal beauty.

Even though the city was abandoned five hundred years before they arrived, the Aztecs tried to reestablish Teotihuacán as a spiritual center. Almost certainly sacrifices similar to those in the Templo Mayor took place here.

Slowly Andrew and I climb the Pyramid of the Sun. Slowly, because the stairs are crowded and dangerous, like the entrance to a

beehive on a summer day. The plains around us look desolate, covered with untended cornfields. Far-away Mexico City glitters sullenly in the shadow of Mount Popocatépetl. I clutch tightly to the rope that cuts the staircase in two parts, an indispensable precaution if you don't want to end up accidentally sacrificed to the sun god.

Without asking me, an old Mexican grabs my arm. He is so old, he looks like a rusty nail. His wobbly legs force me to slow down even more. Behind me, tourists, French, mutter and sigh impatiently. Hanging on to me tighter and tighter, the old man tells me the story of the sun god. At no moment saying "legend." No, it's story or history. For him, the sun god is a fact as well documented as Caesar crossing the Rubicon or Napoleon at Waterloo. He depicts Aztec mythology like a very complicated family saga, as a celestial soap opera where everybody sleeps with everybody else, preferably their mothers or brothers.

The story of the sun's birth, as he tells it, is a feast of divine lunacy: The goddess Coatlicue, after giving birth to her daughter the moon (Coyolzauhaui) and to the rest of the Milky Way, decided, rather un-derstandably, to retire from anymore exertion, and spent the rest of her days napping. One day, as she lay sleeping on the top of a moun-tain, she was fertilized by the feather of a magical bird (her story any-how). Of course nobody believed her, especially her daughters, the moon and the stars. The moon, afraid to lose the title of mommy's fa-vorite daughter, decided to kill her mother; the star sisters agreed. But the magical bird who had lost his feather, who had fertilized Coatlicue (follow me closely here) warned the fetus inside the goddess' womb about his future siblings' intentions. When the moon and the stars ar-rived to execute their mother, *kazam!* The sun jumped out of her

womb (don't ask me how) and cut his sister the moon in two pieces. The stars, not very bravely, screamed and ran away. The baby sun (his name is Huitzilopochtli) condemned his sister the moon to appear complete, in her initial shape, only a few nights a month.

I listen, entranced, to the old man. Everything is in the story: The immaculate conception, the feather that fertilizes the mother's womb (the dove, Holy Spirit, isn't far), and the magnificent allegory of the sun chasing the moon, stars, and darkness away. Stephen Hawking never thought of it.

We are nearly at the top, and my new friend says (I still don't know his name), "Well, when we get our girls pregnant, we are mad at them, we beat them. Still, strange things do happen. Look at the Aztec Mother, look at Nuestra Señora de Guadalupe. They got pregnant without sin, didn't they? This type of thing occurs; one should think about it."

He shakes his head twice, makes a little click with his tongue, and walks away, then disappears at the peak of the building. I look for him several times but never see him again. I didn't even have the chance to thank him for his story.

Even peeled like an onion, the top of the Pyramid of the Sun is still awe inspiring. The crowd, noisy up until now, suddenly falls silent. At the exact top, which looks like a stack of charcoal, a group of expensively dressed American tourists open their arms in devotion to the sun god. Their gestures are wooden, theatrical, and lack any irony; someone must have told them there's a vortex here. A girl talking of Sedona ("It's so amazing!") confirms my worst fears. The only thing that's missing is Yma Sumac's music.

"Let's wait," Andrew says. "In a few minutes, one of them is going to channel Montezuma."

For years, when I lived in the Bay Area, I met an impressive number of Ramses IIs, Rumis, Cleopatras, and one John the Baptist (much dimmed down by successive lives and far more accommodating to life's pleasures and luxuries). I never met anyone who had been a peasant or farmer or carpenter or bricklayer in Luxor. Where do all the working classes go when they reincarnate? As for the channelers I was forced to encounter, channeling Montezuma would be small beer for most of them. One in Santa Cruz claimed the Virgin herself spoke through him whenever and wherever he asked her. Another used to appear with dreadful poems dictated by Rumi, Mirabai, or Hafiz—or sometimes all three—the night before, asking us, of course, to ensure that a major firm published them.

The fake devotion repels me: I know that the top of the pyramid is an outdoor museum, but it's also a sacred place in which terrible things happened. *Terribilis locus iste*—This is a terrible place. That was carved at the entrance to Roman cemeteries. A minute of shattered silence would be more appropriate here, where hundreds of thousands of victims were slaughtered, often with horrifyingly ingenious brutality.

Teotihuacán's little museum contains a few artifacts, most of them copies. The originals are in the museum of anthropology in Mexico City or scattered around the world. Many of them testify eloquently to the mastery of the Aztec craftspeople. Hairpieces made of blue feathers of the quetzal or ctinga bird, human skulls encrusted painstakingly with turquoises and obsidian, knives decorated with lacy filigree mosaics, a magnificent fan also made of feathers and covered with butterflies that could fly immediately from Teotihuacán to one of Lalique's glass fantasies. Besides these, nothing, apart from some beautifully reconstituted frescoes that were discovered on the site.

The museum is a lovely tourist trap. Ahead of us, a darling old German lady with blue hair wonders aloud how a civilization could create such beauty while sacrificing children regularly ("Poor little children!"), forgetful that she comes from a civilization that engendered, in almost the same generation, Rilke and Hitler.

It is a cliché to say that the Aztecs were a paradoxical group, at once fierce warriors and the makers of some of the most dazzlingly delicate poetry ever written about the natural world. Always at war with somebody, they had become, in less than ninety years, the masters of the valley of Mexico, leaving far behind other Meso-American tribes less adroit than they at the art of war. The last emperor himself, Motecuhzuma Xocoyotzin ("angry Lord"; "Montezuma" is a misspelling that can be traced to the first Spanish codices), was apparently both a ferocious warrior and a passionate gardener, whose love of exotic and fragrant rare flowers the Spanish found effeminate.

Bernal Diaz del Castillo, a tough old conquistador in Cortés's troupe, left a description of his first walks in the parks of "the city precious as jade":

> I never tired of noticing the diversity of trees and the various scents given off by each, and the paths choked with roses and other flowers, and the many local fruit trees, and the ponds of fresh water. Everything was shining and decorated with dif-

ferent kinds of stonework and painting that were a marvel to gaze on. Then there were birds of many breeds and varieties that came to drink at the pond.

Cortés had left Vera Cruz with two-thirds of his troops (around four hundred people), with the goal of conquering the Aztec capital. En route they were stopped by a group of warriors, Tlaxcalans, a tribe who had kept their independence from the Aztecs. The Tlaxcalans were soon conquered by the Spanish cannons, and they turned traitor and joined the Spaniards. It's likely that they were thrilled to sabotage the Aztecs. They offered help to Cortés and even guided him through the labyrinths of the forest toward Tenochtitlán.

It is at this moment in the story that Marina, "La Machciche," appears, an Indian girl who could speak Spanish and Nahuatl and who provided Cortés with psychological ruses—and much more, if you believe gossip—that helped him conquer Motecuhzuma. La Machciche is still controversial today. For some, she is the traitoress who sold out her own people; for others, she is a heroine and spared them an even more bloody fate, believing that what she was doing was the right thing. What fate on earth, however, could be more cruel than the one that in the end struck them? In the statue of her I had seen in the wax museum, she had wild, tumbling Ava Gardner hair and flaming red skirts, but a blank stare, as if she had already seen far too much.

Cortés arrived on the shores of Mexico in 1519. The greatest cities of the Old World—Rome, Venice, London, Seville—didn't number more than one hundred thousand people; when Cortés arrived, Tenochtitlán's population was two hundred thousand. Discovering that must have been very humbling for the Spaniards; these were, after all, "barbarians" whose existence wasn't even mentioned in the Bible— proof of their inferiority, or worse.

The first meeting between Cortés and the emperor happened in a strangely friendly way, even if Cortés was to commit a major faux pas when he tried to hug the monarch; two guards seized him and pushed him back brusquely. The same thing would happen today to somebody with the weird idea of embracing Elizabeth II. The Spanish soldiers, not appearing in any way like invaders, were offered princely rooms and treated like visiting officials. This honeymoon lasted less than a week. Cortés heard of an insurrection in Vera Cruz that had cost him several men. This gave him a good excuse to seize the Emperor as a hostage in reprisal.

The Aztecs then saw their reigning god walking down the streets, thankfully not covered with chains but simply surrounded by armed Spanish soldiers. "And as the Aztecs' ruler was led through the streets, he told his agitated people that he was going of his own free will. From then on, Motecuhzuma was little more than a pitiable reciter of proclamations, a ruler in name only while Cortés pulled his strings," writes Frederick Peterson.

How strange that an entire grand, exotic, sophisticated civilization with a large army submitted to a handful of adventurers. Spanish fire power is not an adequate explanation. The most believable theory derives, strangely, from the occult beliefs that ruled the Aztecs.

Perhaps each civilization has its Achilles heel through which destroying, dissolving forces can enter. Perhaps the Aztecs' was their overintense faith in the world of omens and signs and dreams. Years earlier, the emperor's sister had had a dream of white men coming from across the sea and inaugurating a new era that would coincide with the end of the Aztecs. Motecuhzuma himself was obsessed by a prediction of the imminent return of Quetzalcoatl, the feathered snake, who had left earth long before. He was supposed to come back on a ship that would spit the fire of the gods. The legend made it clear that no one should even try to oppose him or the destruction to follow. It was the divine order that the Aztecs were to disappear.

The most bizarre of all ironies is that the arrival of the Spaniards coincided with the year Quetzalcoatl was fated to return, according to the Aztec calendar. No wonder then that Motecuhzuma did so extraordinarily little to oppose what he must have seen as the unfolding of the divine will. In a strange, almost macabre way, he actually helped the invaders, relaying faithfully their commands to his people while being sure he was accomplishing heaven's will.

Motecuhzuma wasn't simply the victim of his own religious fantasy. Many signs had preceded the Spaniards, enough evidence for a superstitious civilization that their time had come: According to an Aztec codex, a "tongue of fire" appeared above the Templo Mayor not long before the Spaniards invaded. The next day, the sun didn't rise, and the light was ash-colored for hours. A little later, another temple burned down without any reason, and a comet appeared in the middle of the afternoon. A column of fire turned around the Templo Mayor for hours, and the Texcoco lake suddenly flooded the whole area, destroying crops, without any excessive rain to explain its behavior.

The night before Cortés entered Tenochtitlán, the voice of a woman was heard crying, "My children, we must leave. Where could we go?" The voice seemed to be coming from the sky itself. From that moment everything went terribly wrong—or right, according to the prophecies. A testimony of this time, the Cédula Real, tells us that "many Indians hung themselves, others let themselves die of hunger, others poisoned themselves with sacred herbs; there are mothers who kill their children to whom they have just given birth, saying that they are doing it to spare them the trials that they are enduring."

The emperor, now just a puppet of the conquerors, bade farewell to his people. He had tried to escape, but his priests convinced him to stay and fulfill his destiny. A friar who witnessed the last public appearance of Motecuhzuma wrote that "with abundant tears, he cried out to the masses that he was terrified about the arrival of the strangers. Afterwards, he bade farewell to his wives and children with sorrows and tears, charging all his attendants to care for his family, since he considered himself a man about to die."

Nobody was to see the emperor alive again. Thirty years later, secure in his gentleman-scholar's tower, Montaigne wrote about Motecuhzuma's end and gave him a death scene that the emperor himself could have appreciated:

And the king of Mexico defended his city with the perseverance and bravery of a prince ... The Spaniards didn't find the gold that they had dreamed of. They condemned the king and the principal lords of his court to die. The king and his servants were laid on a burning charcoal bed. One servant, turning his head toward his sovereign, asked him for mercy. The king fixed fiercely his eyes on him and, reproaching him his cowardice, told him, "Am I in a rosewater bath? Are you better than I am?"

The truth, however, is less grand. The emperor probably died like a dog, stoned to death by Spanish soldiers. Other sources relate that he was stabbed in the back, the punishment destined for traitors.

Astonished by the image on the peasant's rough cloth, Bishop Zumárraga falls on his knees and begs Juan Diego for his forgiveness. He invites him to stay a few days. The Tilma is kept in the prelate's private chapel.

The day after, the bishop asks Juan Diego to show him the sites of the apparitions. "Let's go and see where it is the will of the Lady from heaven that her hermitage be built." The construction of the shrine starts almost immediately.

Juan Diego returns to his hamlet to visit his uncle. He doesn't need to hurry, certain that old Bernardino has been cured. When he arrives, already surrounded by believers and the freshly converted, he finds his uncle in vibrant health and surprised to see his nephew, the object of so much honor and attention. Don Bernardino tells Juan Diego the whole story, how the Virgin of Tepeyac also appeared to him, told him not to worry, explained why Juan Diego wasn't back yet, and—the best part—healed him miraculously.

Nephew and uncle head back to the city. They are going to be the bishop's guests. On the twenty-sixth of December, less than three weeks after the first apparition, the first chapel of Tepeyac, the Ermita, is inaugurated. The Tilma is taken to it that very day. Several churches have been built since then on Tepeyac, but the Tilma has never left the site for long.

In the bus back to Mexico City, shaken by the dirt roads, stopping every five minutes to pick up people in the same dusty-gray concrete villages, I reread the admirable translations of Aztec poetry of Miguel León-Portilla:

> Only from his home do they come, from the innermost part of
>    Heaven.
> Only from these comes a myriad of flowers . . .
> Where the nectar of the flowers is found
> The fragrant beauty of the flower is refined . . .
> They interlace, they interweave;
> Among them sing, among them warbles the quetzal bird.

And this one, attributed to an ancient king, Nezhualcoyotl, worthy of the greatest Chinese Zen poets or Basho himself, that sums up all the sadness of the end of the Aztecs:

> Is it true that on earth one lives?
> Not forever on earth, only a little while
> Though jade it may be, it breaks:
> Though gold it may be, it is crushed:
> Though it be quetzal plumes, it shall not last
> Not forever on earth, only a little while.

The stage was set for the arrival of Guadalupe. She was supposed to heal the past and give birth to a glorious future. But did she? The despair of every conceivable kind and shape that I see around her basilica or on the faces of the young and old on TV, trying every day to smuggle themselves across the tortilla curtain near San Diego, toward the new promised land; doesn't this go on echoing the ancient and terrible humiliation of the Aztecs? Wasn't it this humiliation and its effects the Virgin promised to transform? So many promises. Lanore's caustic, agonized voice and words return to me in waves. What would the poor and oppressed and despairing do without Guadalupe? And what difference does she really make?

I sit glumly at the bus window as it stops at yet another of the desolate and faceless villages that surround Mexico City. Four thin, mangy dogs quarrel over a decaying dead goat as a newspaper blows chaotically down the deserted, sun-baked central street out of an early de Chirico. An old woman sits in a doorway, her rosary lying unused in her lap, her eyes two dark pools of misery and resignation. In front of her, a half-naked little girl plays ball slowly, as if in a trance.

Next day, Sunday. In the morning, before going to the basilica, we decide to walk to the flower market at the end of our *calle.*

The large warehouse seems to be the only thing open in the deserted streets, lined by houses with their blinds firmly drawn down. Inside, many of the booths are closed. Slowly, however, the dealers start opening up shop, calling from one stand to another, laughing and joking. The stark smell of detergent mingles with the pungent scent of fish of all sizes sprawled on a vast table covered with ice, large as a frozen pond.

Near one of the entrances there's a butcher's shop with ziggurats of meat whose blatant red is exaggerated by pink neon lights like those in Amsterdam brothels. An old woman with a blue bandanna around her forehead sits behind the towers of skinned corpses, reading a *fotonovela*. On the cover, a Dolores Del Rio look-alike in a black cocktail dress with several pearl necklaces swoons into the arms of a dashing middle-aged gangster type with whitened temples and a gun bulging out of his right tuxedo pocket. Without saying a word, her eyes rapt, the old woman waves her right hand lazily from time to time to shoo away the flies.

Above the stacks of too-red meat stands La Lupe, nearly life-size, in aging blotchy plastic, with a full regalia of red and white false carnations and flashing blue, pink, and green Christmas lights. Blood drips drop by drop onto the freshly washed white tiles beneath her. I think of something Kate Simon wrote: "Some of us are appalled at the cruelty to dogs in Mexico, though they are skinny, yellow curs, poison-colored and the shape of death. Mexicans are appalled at the harsh piercing voices we sometimes use with our children. To them, this is a great cruelty."

For centuries, every autumn, thousands of goats were sacrificed in a ritual *matanza,* or slaughter. Until recently, the animals were hung up by the rear feet, throat only slightly slit open, so the blood could drip slowly. This was considered the best way to get the richest meat. In the early eighties the animal-rights activists succeeded in having a law passed that forbids the slitting of the goat's throat. Nowadays the goats are shot in the head. In large cities, anyway.

For centuries, too, the *matanceros* have offered their murders to the Virgin. They prepare a special dish with *mole,* that incomparable spiced sauce. It's apparently a very difficult dish to get right; it takes hours of work. The *matanza* coincides with harvest time; what is it but an always-repeated fertility rite, the eternally renewed bloody gratitude for the fresh crops, offered to Tonantzin or Guadalupe (the same goddess under different names), while the blood of goats runs on the hacienda's floors for weeks, like the menstrual blood of the planet.

"Goat very bad," a middle-aged butcher with a thin white mustache tells me. We have just been talking about the *matanza,* and he can see clearly my lack of cultural understanding. "Goats very bad."

"Why?"

He smiles broadly and the one gold tooth in the front of his mouth glitters in the pink neon lights. "In the country, they . . . you know . . . they eat marijuana fields . . . all the buds . . . terrible. After, they are very, very *wild.*"

A woman who must be in her late eighties is setting up her flower booth, ringed by orange buckets nearly as tall as she is. She is bowed down by age and arthritis and moves surreally slowly, talking serenely to herself. As I get closer, I notice she is wearing a bright pink serape. A serape is the modern form of the *tilma* that Juan Diego wore. When I tell her that I intend to take her flowers to the Virgin in the basilica, she pays special attention to them and insists on me inspecting every stem. Her little store looks like an explosion in a paint factory. We pick some half-opened gladiolus. "Good," she approves. I want to add some tuberoses but the old lady says firmly, "No. They cost a fortune." I think to myself if it were for my girlfriend, it would be okay, but it's too gaudy and showy for La Virgen. As she finishes the bouquet, singing a little under her breath, she adds two stems of pink daylilies. She makes us understand that it's from her, *"por la Madre."*

We go out and stop at Lucinda's for breakfast, or rather for what she will deign to give us. Lucinda is beautiful, around sixty, very fat, with the rakish face of a gypsy and fierce emerald eyes. Ava Gardner on steroids. She runs her little cantina at her own very personal rhythm, adoring some walk-ins and summarily ushering out others for reasons known only to her.

From the first day, she decides that we are "okay" (her ultimate compliment). After she watches us drink our first (terrible) cup of coffee without complaining, she decrees that we are "her sons." You don't always get what you've ordered at Lucinda's; the menu is as unreliable as the Mexican legal system, but a cup of coffee can come with a huge plate of fried bananas soaked in honey or *arroz almendadro* that Lucinda forgets to mention on the check. A chain-smoker, she scratches her hair above her stove—and what hair! Blond at the ends, beyond about an inch of gray.

I have been wanting to meet a *bruja,* a white witch. Lucinda knows one and is going to introduce me, her son, to someone she calls (crossing herself) "the wise woman of Guadalupe," who practices healing magic in the name (and with the help) of La Madre.

"She doesn't want to be called *bruja.* Say *curandera* instead," Lucinda whispers, enunciating each syllable exaggeratedly as if I were her deaf three-year-old.

She hesitated a long time before agreeing to introduce me to a *bruja.* One definition of a *bruja,* as I've said, is a woman of Guadalupe, a white witch. She is also very often a midwife, a healer, a confessor. A shrink, too, for the women in remote villages who never talk to anybody. Lucinda thought about my request for days, as if I had asked for her daughter's hand. Now she has made an appointment.

Lucinda lights three cigarettes at the same time and stuffs one each in our mouths, each filter ringed by the mark of her fuchsia lipstick.

"Okay, *muchachos,* no bread today. I have some *pollo* left over from yesterday. Very good."

Chicken. For breakfast. It's only eight in the morning, but we are, after all, at Lucinda's.

She comes back with a plate of fish doughnuts, sort of beignets, and two cups of coffee so strong they look solid. "Some pomegranate to take home?" Without waiting for an answer, she puts it on the table, wrapped in the pages of a Mexican film magazine.

"Going to the football game this afternoon?" she asks.

"No, we are going to La Villa."

She signs. "I'm going. *Mi amante* is playing."

Lucinda has a lover. A skinny little man in his twenties, yellow-skinned and always vaguely scared-looking. I have never heard his voice. My poor Spanish is not the reason. Even with Lucinda, he just nods and grins uneasily. Their age difference, which is *grande,* doesn't affect Lucinda in the least, who talks openly about their nights with dreamy eyes, nearly breathless.

She ignores the two German tourists who have come in and called to her her a dozen times. They leave, and she watches them go with a smile. Then she sits down at our table and sighs again and lights yet another cigarette, having lost the other one. After two or three puffs, she announces calmly, "*Mi abuela* . . . my grandmother . . . she saw La Guadalupe."

I jump. "But Lucinda, you never told me that!"

"Well, you never asked me!" She goes on. "Abuelita, she was *encinta,* pregnant. It wasn't the first time. She had carried a lot of babies, all stillborn . . . they would die in her belly. So this time, she went to the basilica, she walked to the altar and said, *"Madre,* if this one comes dead, I'll kill myself, it's that simple!"

It seems to me that her *abuelita* was using a rather earthy form of blackmail, but what can you hope for from Lucinda's grandmother?

Lucinda pauses for dramatic effect, puffing out perfect rings of smoke with long-practiced mastery. "Later that day," she continues, "my grandmother was praying in her bedroom. She had to get up; the rose perfume around her was getting so intense she just knew something was going on!"

She takes another puff, then looks at her empty cup and yells something in the direction of the kitchen. Mi Amante appears, trembling, with a coffeepot.

"And then?" I risk.

Lucinda looks at me like a lawyer announcing to a group of heirs the demise of a rich uncle. "And then she looked up, and there was Guadalupe, floating in the bedroom!"

"Wow, Lucinda, this is great material! She saw Guadalupe!"

"Yes!"

"How was she?"

"What do you mean, how was she? She was the Virgin! She looked very nice, very proper, just like herself!"

"What did she say?"

"She told Abuelita that she was going to have a nice baby. 'You'll have your baby,' she said, 'a big baby boy,' and *pschuit,* she disappeared! But the smell of roses remained; all the neighbors came and smelled it! And later, when my father was born, they named him Juan Diego!"

She pauses, happy with the end of her speech. She looks at the empty cups, then sighs and seems to decide the kitchen is too far away at the moment to bother to clear the table.

"Abuelita, she went to the Villa every Sunday, all her life. She never missed one. Not a single one. She died in 1982. Cancer. Two days before, she asked me to take her to the Tilma. I carried her and they stopped the escalators for a minute, for her to stand without falling down. It was her last Sunday and on Tuesday, she died, *pschuit!*"

She rises and comes back with the *pollo,* served on two gaudily decorated nonmatching plates. She arranges the silverware on the side of my plate and picks pensively at a slice of fried zucchini.

"And look at that bastard!"

"What bastard?"

"My father. Nuestra Señora came especially to announce his birth! And what is he doing now? He is a drunk, he gambles, and he goes to porn movies! At eighty-four!"

When we arrive at the basilica, we realize that the whole Villa, as well as the plaza that contains the two basilicas fenced with tall, yellow grilles, is closed, surrounded by a belt of policemen holding hands, who are trying to contain the crowd's enthusiasm and stop it from coming in. I virtually swim my way through the throng—thanks to my elbows—and ask a policeman what all the hoopla is about. For a moment, I think there might have been a bombing. There is always a bomb ready to explode somewhere in Mexico.

"The doors will open in fifteen minutes," the policeman tells me. That's around three-quarters of an hour in Mexico time.

For the first time since I arrived in Mexico City, I feel scared. I have been warned about the cab drivers that take you to a dark suburb and cut your throat, about the filthy water, the scorpions under the pillows, the curses of the begging witches you ignore, the absence of the mystical power of Visa cards in many places. But no one has told me about the crowd. The "holy" crowd, the crowd of the children of Guadalupe, the ones I mentally called my brothers and sisters while reading the literature of the apparitions. And now, here I am, at the core of something that breathes like one single chest, up and down, up and down. I could drown and nobody would see. I cannot move my arms; I can barely breathe. I follow what seems to be a general direction, as though all these lives assembled here are proceeding forward on two gigantic feet.

The whole of Mexico City is around me—old Indian women with leathery faces, moving like jaguars; preppy young men overperfumed and trying hard to look American; beggars of all ages; children and older people in wheelchairs; teenagers showing off their muscles; big women with Sunday clothes and immobile, architectural hair; bankers with long ebony canes and slicked-back Valentino hair. I suppose this universality is one of the miracles of La Lupe: I have visited most of the Marian sites around the world—Lourdes, Fátima, Beauraing—and in all these places, the pilgrims have a kind of family resemblance, something in their look that links them, though not necessarily flattering, but real, a family aura. Not here. Here everyone flaunts his or her differences. The Virgin welcomes everyone without exception, under the moon crescent where her feet rest.

A growl of engines comes closer and closer. The crowd parts like the Red Sea, to make way for a number of enormous Harley-Davidsons commanded by big, bearded guys, some wearing shirts with skull-and-crossbones and on the back the announcement: "If you can read this, the bitch fell off."

"Oh, yes," chirps a woman next to me, "today's the bikers' pilgrimage."

The machines are magnificent. I have never seen more Harleys in such good condition, so lovingly kept. They glitter in the morning sun, and many carry a life-size Guadalupe made of real and fake flowers, three-dimensional. The face is composed of pale-pink carnations, the green dress formed by ferns, the stars are daisies or mums, all covering a dress dummy or something human shaped. They are bizarrely beautiful. One is covered with electric Christmas garlands directly connected to the motorcycle battery. When the biker presses on the pedal, Guadalupe lights up like a Vegas billboard.

Next to the Villa, where the human tide is right now taking me, is a desolate little field surrounded by corrugated iron walls, where the floral tributes of past Sundays are decaying. Headless Virgins are propped up against others who have lost their arms or legs. A heavy smell of decomposition floats around the graveyard of Guadalupes, each one bearing names of local banks, bus or insurance companies, hotels, and restaurants. In Mexico, each firm or organization sends its own special float on its own special Sunday to procure the Virgin's protection.

The crowd's pressure is getting crazier by the minute, the policemen look at each other, hoping that one of them will make a decision.

But what decision? The flowers I've been holding since my arrival look as if they have been pressed fiercely between two phone books; only the pink lilies of the old woman of the market have resisted so far. Despite the madness, a woman next to me calmly kneels. Her hair is so sleek and dark it looks like the shining ebony of a concert Steinway. One by one, she takes out little packages rolled in newspaper from her bag, uncovering chopped onion, sliced tomatoes, Rona bread, and green peppers cut thin like transparent jade. Slowly, almost ritualistically, she fixes tacos and hands them to her family gathered around her.

Suddenly, the police walkie-talkies explode with commands like a mountain dam that breaks. The large yellow grille opens creakingly and the crowd spills suddenly into the plaza like quicksilver. Without realizing it, I find myself standing at the door of the old basilica next to a sweating fat woman wearing a shirt with a picture of Tom Cruise. She seems to be enjoying herself. "Fun, no?" She smiles at me. She tears off a large piece of bread from the loaf she is carrying and gives it to an old man I have noticed before. He is gaunt, with a razor-thin face and oddly exalted eyes, like a figure out of El Greco. She turns to me and says, "When I gave him the bread, he told me he had just asked the Virgin for lunch, and now she had given it to him." The woman with the Tom Cruise shirt wipes a tear from her eye. "She is our mother."

Her simple words shake me, and once again the miracle of Guadalupe—that she appeared here and has remained physically present on the Tilma, like a miraculous Polaroid, inspiring God only knows how many daily miracles of every kind—brings me mentally to my knees.

The bishop at last appears, surrounded by a chorus line of men in black. Dressed in violent shades of red, he seems surprisingly young to be a bishop. He blesses babies and holds the tips of my fingers, calls me *amigo.* Close up, he looks like Desi Arnaz, but his smile is less open: the face of a master diplomat, too suave for my taste.

Pausing on the steps, he sweeps into the basilica and a crowd runs after him. I stay outside with a thousand others. The bishop starts the mass. Each time his voice buzzes and crackles from the gigantic speakers at each side of the square, the human sea cheers and whistles like they would for a rock band.

I can finally sit on the steps of the old basilica. I open the wonderful book of Virgil Elizondo, *Guadalupe: A Mother for the New Creation*:

Mount Tepeyac takes its place among the famous mountains of God's saving history: It is the Mount Sinai of the Americas, for it is here that God gives the new law of love, protection and compassion for the people. It is the Mount of the beatitudes of the Americas, for through the relationship and conversation between the Lady and Juan Diego, we can hear and experience a blessing pronounced on the poor, the meek, the lowly, the sorrowing, the peacemakers and the persecuted of the New World. It is the mountain of the Transfiguration of the Americas, for here the glory of God is clearly manifested to God's chosen one, Juan Diego.

With these words ringing in my heart, I walk into the large chapel next to the old basilica. I look around. Old ladies are kissing the glass coffin where another large wax Christ gazes out in agony. They rub small candles on their foreheads or anywhere on the bodies of the children with them, before lighting them, a strange ritual that makes them intermediaries of the divine power. And who knows, perhaps it is a way also of ensuring that the blessing they hunger for really works.

Kneeling, I think suddenly of the old man who accepted the piece of bread a few minutes ago outside the church. He knew the Virgin would provide him a lunch. He surely didn't know how, when, or what, but he *knew* he was going to be fed immediately. My inner skeptic asks, Why then doesn't she help him with more than just a loaf of cheap bread? Why does she let him age and wither in the street, where he will undoubtedly also die? But then, to accept poverty with the radiant face of the old man may well be the greatest of miracles.

I open Elizondo again:

The grace and allurement of our Lady offers also a parallel to those offered by Jesus. Jesus attracted the poor, the hopeless and the marginals of his time not by criticizing them or by belittling their religious practices or by threatening them with hell. Jesus brought good news to the poor, sight to the blind, and liberty to the captives. That is why he was so attractive to the masses of damned humanity, and so repulsive to the religiously correct people of his time. Guadalupe is just like that. And to [them] she continues to be alluring, calling all the hurting, disfigured and disinherited to herself. "Come to me all of you who are tired and weary, and I will refresh you." Her gentleness, evident concern, and compassionate love are the source of her recreating power.

I walk out. The blinding silver light and noisy, ebullient crowd climbing Tepeyac (Elizondo's "masses of damned humanity" in their

Sunday best) are shocking for someone coming out of the serene bluish womb of the small chapel. I buy a dozen candles wrapped in cardboard cones. The old man who sells them asks me if I want "girls." Since his tables are covered with religious knickknacks, I am certain I misheard him. Then he asks me one more time if I want "girls" while handing me the flyer of a strip club. The Club Jet Set. I don't want to offend him or to appear holier-than-thou, so I study the flyer assiduously for a moment before handing it back to him.

"No girls today," I say, *"por la Virgen."*

He shrugs and rolls his eyes.

I go and sit on the steps of the new basilica, and at the bottom of every candle, I carve the name of a friend, dead or alive, for whom I will pray when I light it. I always pray for others before asking for myself. Nothing to do with holiness; no, asking for others gives me the feeling I am cheating on God, making Him believe I am much better than I am so he will grant my own secret request faster. I developed this technique of blackmail when I was nine years old, tormented by the perverse Catholic cult of selflessness. It's a hard habit to break.

As I enter the basilica, I buy a tiny bouquet of honeysuckle. The perfume makes me so joyful I eat a blossom. The old nun with the bulldog face is still at the door, inspecting the pilgrims with her gimlet gaze. The melody *"pesopesopeso"* and the smell of fried *gorditas* dance in the hot air. For some reason, these words from Revelation that I have always loved and identified with Guadalupe spring up in my mind:

And a great sign appeared in Heaven,
a woman clothed with the sun

And the moon under her feet
And upon her head, a crown of twelve stars
And being with child
She cried out in her travail
and was in the anguish of delivery.

Looking around at all the faces painted with hope and misery, I think suddenly that the passage should read, "and being with children."

I remember my stupefaction at seeing for the first time an amazing Madonna with Child of the Lima School, at the Dominique du Mesnil Museum in Houston: The baby Jesus sticks his head out between two pleats of Mary's dress that very clearly evoke a vagina. Suddenly I notice I am surrounded by pregnant women, at least a dozen of them. I feel dizzy as I walk to a bench in the center of the basilica, now deserted by most of its morning crowd.

I open my copy of Elizondo one last time:

Our Lady of Guadalupe is not just another Marian apparition. Guadalupe has to do with the core of the gospel itself. It is nothing less than an original American gospel, a narrative of the birth/resurrection experience at the very beginning of the crucifixion of the natives, the African and mestizo and mulatto children. Guadalupe is the most prodigious event since the coming of our lord and savior, Jesus Christ. Her compassionate *rostro y corazón* [countenance and heart] are alive not only on the Tilma, but also in the faces and hearts of all who see her, call upon her and believe in her. She is here among us, and when we need her.

Was there ever an age when we needed her more?

The bishop is gone now, and the bikers are leaving. In the open plaza a few middle-aged women start slowly to dance in a circle. One stops near me with a flower tiny as a shirt button behind her ear. The circle keeps growing and growing, adding people of all ages with every loop. It soon turns into a human maelstrom, but undangerous in its swirling, even benevolent.

With a few high tenor and soprano voices leading, everyone starts to sing a song like a primitive lullaby. I can recognize the words, "We are your children, you are the mother and the queen." Very soon, what begins as a ballad turns into a dazzling flamenco, and the whole square becomes a ballroom. I sit back on the steps. The circle is still getting larger and now covers the whole plaza. The rhythm gets faster and faster, and so do the words. The dancing ends with a flurry of "*¡Viva!*" and all the people raise their arms to the skies for almost a minute in a tribal communion surely far older than the events of Tepeyac.

After a minute of almost surreal silence, familiar noises break out again. On the steps of the new basilica, two women—rosary dealers— are viciously fighting, scratching, kicking each other in the stomach, punching each other in the nose. Several men cluster around, mockingly egging them on, as in a *corrida*. Two policemen gaze at the scene passively, visibly aroused by the naked flesh that jumps from unbuttoned blouses. A priest finally appears and separates the two viragos, who keep on screaming, cursing, and spitting.

"Yes," sighs the fat woman in the Tom Cruise shirt, who sits down next to me. "La Señora has a lot to do."

Lucinda has left me a message at the hotel. When I arrive at the cantina, she is sitting at a table in a yellow-gold blouse, imperial like a vain customer who disapproves of the stained tablecloth.

"Coffee?" she almost barks.

"Yes. You wanted to see me?"

"Yes. Milk?"

"Yes. Is it about the *bruja*?"

"Yes. But you won't say '*bruja*.' You'll say '*curandera*.' Sugar?"

"No. Thanks. It's about the *curandera*?"

"Yes." She hands me twenty pesos. "Go and buy me cigarettes across the street. I'm gonna start to heat up the *sopa*, and you'll eat with me."

I bring back the cigarettes. As always, she lights two at the same time and sticks one in my mouth. Today her lipstick is poppy red.

"My friend Rosaria will receive you tomorrow. You will say Doña Rosaria, right? Two o'clock. Be on time."

As she talks to me, she readjusts one of her fake eyelashes, looking at her large reflection in a knife blade.

"Is she a *bruja*?"

"*Curandera*. If you call her *bruja*, she will poison you."

"But *bruja* is a good word, no?"

"It *was* a good word. Words are good, people are bad. *Brujería* is good; but nowadays, people mix *brujería* and black magic. That's why she doesn't want to be called a *bruja*."

Lucinda gives up her battle with her eyelashes.

"Rosaria's father was an Indian. He talked with animals and with the gods. He was an *adivino* from the Tepehua tribe. Her mother had the power too. She could heal people just by blowing on them! Rosaria has the same power. She prays. She burns candles. She burns the red candle to call up the power, and she helps a lot of people! Marina, Pico's mother [Pico being Mi Amante], she says that if she can take away evil, she can bring it in too, but when she's mad at me, she says that I've seen a *diablera* to get Mi Amante."

She touches her cleavage with a fingertip, as though applying a rare perfume. "I never needed a *diablera* to keep a man. Never."

Lucinda reigns, quiet, matriarchal, among all this dysfunction and emotional chaos, playing at the same time best friend and daughter-in-law of a woman ten years younger than she, who also is her lover's mother.

"Have you seen a lot of *curanderos* in your life?"

Lucinda blows her smoke toward a fly without any result, since the fly comes back instantly.

"It's cheaper than the doctor and it works better. It's the Madre and the saints that do the work. No pills."

"Are *curanderos* omnipotent?"

She looks at me with disdain, the heaviness of her look accentuated by the rebellious eyelashes.

"God is omnipotent. We do what we can."

"You have the proof of their powers then?"

"Proof? What proof? Everybody knows it works! Nobody needs proof! You go to the *herbario* [herbalist] and then you go to the *curandero*, and next moon, *pschuit!* Finish! My friend Rosaria has cured another friend, Dolores, from kidney failure. She had seen every doctor in Mexico! Even the doctors of Durango could not do a thing! [For Lucinda, doctors from Durango are a class apart. Below the *curandero*, of course, but the *crème de la crème* when it comes to physicians.] Rosaria, she prayed during the changes of the moon, she has given a medal of San Martín de Porres to Dolores, and some *barba de maíz* [cornsilk tea] to drink and *pschuit!* Finish with kidney failure! Dolores's husband was so thrilled that he gave her a new set of teeth, all in gold. Dolores has made a grotto in her garden now for La Señora de Guadalupe and San Martín de Porres, the Santo Niño . . . She is furious because the cats go to sleep in the grotto, but I told her that it was good, that her cats were *católicos.*"

Lucinda pours boiling water in my cup, then adds a huge tablespoon of instant coffee. She scratches her left buttock pensively. "Here is the address. Be there tomorrow at two; don't be late. And no useless words. Don't ask too many questions. *En boca cerrada, no entran moscas.*" Flies, she reminds me, can't enter a closed mouth.

The day after, at one minute before two, I stand at the door of Doña Rosaria. She lives in a little neat building on a calm street not far from the flea market.

A boy of five or six opens the door, looks at me intensely for ten seconds, then shuts it. I knock again; this time it's a plump woman with the same piercing black eyes as the little boy. She looks unnerved.

"Doña Rosaria?"

"*Sí.*" She gives me a look that seems to regret her invitation and curse Lucinda at the same time. "*Sí, norteamericano* . . . come in."

I walk into an apartment with currant-red walls that smell of olive oil. She opens a door at once, as if afraid of showing me anything else of her flat, and she pushes me inside a little room with a table and two chairs. There, an oak stool supports a two-foot statue of Guadalupe with a crown of Christmas glitter. On the other side of the room is something more elaborate, like an altar, where stands Guadalupe, our Lady of Lourdes, and La Purísima, who has been obviously hand-repainted and who has lost her serenity: She is now cross-eyed like Norma Shearer.

Doña Rosaria sits down and with a movement of her chin, indicates that I can sit. She is around forty-five, maybe younger. It's difficult to evaluate age in a culture that ages women so fast. Her hair is black, her eyes are fierce, and her lips are an extravagant red. The lipstick contradicts her severe, judging black eyes; the heavy medal of the sacred heart between her breasts compensates for her rather short brown skirt that just covers her knees.

"What do you want?"

I try to explain; only try, because her "I have tons of other stuff to do than listen to you, jerk" attitude doesn't help the cause of writers lost in suburban Mexico City. Well, where to start? The book, the traditions, Guadalupe?

"Guadalupe? What do you want to write about Guadalupe for? She doesn't need another book."

She gives me no chance to respond.

"And why are you coming to see *me?* Why me?"

She starts to gabble in Spanish. Even though my Spanish isn't good enough to keep up with her, I understand that she is calling down the fires of heaven on Lucinda and her big painted mouth.

"I am nothing special, let alone extraordinary. Just a midwife, nothing else. My family left me some powerful prayers, and I use them to help people—but the Virgin does the work. Big interview for you, hey?"

She puts her hands on her hips and eyes me contemptuously. I wish she'd let me speak, even two lines.

"I have no power," she rasps on, coughing a little. "When you listen to music, are you grateful to the musician or to the technology, the speaker that plays the music? Answer me! Don't waste my time or yours!"

"Well, actually, I am grateful to the musician *and* the speaker—"

"Nahhhh!" she growls, a little put out by my tenacity. Still, she nearly convinces me. The apartment has nothing really witchy about it, no dark bottles containing strange liquors, no black cat, no crystal ball, no skull with popping crystal eyes.

Doña Rosaria reads my mind. "What did you think? I would come and open the door on a broom?"

She seems pretty happy with her *bon mot* and smiles for the first time, displaying rows of dirty teeth with dull gold caps. She stands and walks toward the door, showing me that the museum is closing. Then she stops and turns to me.

"When are you leaving Mexico?"

"Next week."

"When exactly next week?"

"Next Wednesday."

She pauses. "Then come on Sunday. Are you going to the basilica on Sunday?"

"Yes, I go to the basilica every day."

"Okay. Go on Sunday and pray for the sick and come and see me Sunday afternoon, yes, Sunday afternoon. And come alone. No talk to anybody, no camera. Okay?"

Once more I find myself in the deserted street, shaded by tall jacarandas. Why did she change her mind so radically, so fast? I feel torn between my desire to enter the world of *brujería* and the fear of having my throat cut for my credit cards and my watch here in this strange street, or during the appointment with this strange woman of whom I can speak to no one.

Nobody can really understand nor explain the origins of *brujería*. What is almost certain, however, is that the first *brujas* practicing in the name of Guadalupe were ex-priestesses or daughters of priestesses of Tonantzin. The Aztecs, sensitive as they were to the phases of the moon, couldn't forget that all things on earth are driven by the natural forces directly controlled by the divine mother. What the West dismisses as superstition often finds its basis and sometimes part of its truth in many different and ancient traditions, such as Chinese feng shui or the rites of the aborigines. Psychologist Mary Devine, in a chapter of her book *Witches from Guadalupe,* makes this clear:

Aware that they could never eradicate her cult, the Spanish missionaries simply baptized Tonantzin and swathed her in a Christian robe. Then, they sat back and rubbed their hands with glee while the vanquished Aztecs flocked to the shrine.

What the padres didn't know was the fact that Tonantzin wasn't an innocuous run-of-the-mill mother goddess. Under the name of [Tlatzolteotl], "Eater of Filth," she purified sinful humanity via confession to her priests and priestesses, and the priestesses held secret rituals to aid their followers. In other words, they were witches.

"Eater of filth" or "The one who crushes the serpent's head," as she introduced herself to Juan Diego. Do I have a rendezvous with a granddaughter of one of the groupies or with a slightly disturbed woman who has found a way to fight against her boredom and Mexican machismo?

On my way back to the hotel, I stop at Lucinda's. She is feeding Mi Amante, forcing down the throat of the terrified skinny young man huge steaming platters of rice with vegetables.

"Hey, did you see her?"

"Yes, and I will see her again on Sunday."

"Good," says Lucinda. "The saints must have told her you were a good boy. Otherwise she would have thrown you out the window. Did she tell you secrets? Did she show you her grotto? Do you want some *crème caramel*?"

"No," I reply to all three questions, and Lucinda looks slightly offended, probably certain Rosaria has spoken and that I don't want to share what she told me.

"Does she charge, Doña Rosaria? . . . I mean, does she ask for money?"

"No," says Lucinda. "Sometimes she accepts flowers, but often she just wants some food. She'll say, 'Go food shopping for me.' "

This is a good sign, I think. My friend Gabriella, an extraordinary medium, whose gifts have been proven to me a million times, has often told me that people who accept payment for their spiritual services, healing, or prayers, aren't authentic. Or that, if they are, perhaps at the beginning, God takes away the gift because they shouldn't make money out of it. Rosaria is becoming more sympathetic.

Lucinda, by now totally excited over my coming meeting with "her" *bruja,* wants to set the record straight right away. "You will tell in your article that it's thanks to me that you met Rosaria, and then, if it is a success, I will go to New York and Hollywood. I will get everybody and everything I want."

Mi Amante, not at all disturbed—and perhaps relieved—by the idea of Lucinda Superstar, keeps eating, looking always like a frightened rabbit; I don't have the heart to tell Lucinda that the book I am planning isn't the kind to get filmed.

Lucinda suddenly disappears and comes back with two glasses and a bottle of tequila, to show me out of a strange pride or twisted motherliness that only she and I are old enough to drink. She then goes behind the bar and starts to mix two Isabellas, singing out for me the recipe in her cracked contralto:

### Isabella

(per glass)

2 ounces tequila

4 ounces fresh orange juice

Cinnamon to taste

A cloud of nutmeg

Then, while sipping her glass, she greedily begins a swirling litany of macabre, exaggerated stories that seem to have been transmitted by a whole crew of Mexican Edgar Allan Poes. She puts such elan into her recitation that I doubt that this is her first Isabella of the day.

"My friend Dolores—not the Dolores who had bad kidneys, but another Dolores, the one from Durango, well, her family was from Durango. . . . Anyway, her brother was a real drunk! A bastard, just like mine. Anyhow, Dolores decided to go and see the *bruja,* and the *bruja* told her"—here Lucinda sighs noisily and crosses her arms over her chest—"the *bruja* told her to bring her brother to her next full moon.

"Then Dolores spoke to her brother, and she made him swear on a burning red candle"— a second sign of the cross—"not to drink again. And her brother swore, and also to be faithful to his wife. Oh my God, he was ·also going to see *putas.* But then, of course, he started again. He went to the brothel and danced all night like a madman with a beautiful girl. And after, he took her for a moonlit walk in the field— you know, he just wanted to . . ." Here she looks in the direction of Mi Amante just to make me understand that some words are not acceptable in front of little children. ". . . and while walking, he met the *bruja,* who was picking herbs—it's the best time to pick herbs, during the night—well, the *bruja* was very sad and disappointed and she told him, 'You gonna make the Virgin cry,' and the brother of Dolores, he couldn't care less, and he went down to the field with the beautiful *puta.* And when in the grass, he wanted to hold her tighter—you understand what I mean—he looked at her and suddenly he was holding a rotting corpse, covered with fat, juicy worms! Then he ran screaming, and for days, they all thought he was *loco.* But he never touched a glass of alcohol since then. Never!"

Lucinda looks at me, her eyes blazing with self-pleasure, then gulps down the last sip of her Isabella. Licking her lips, she almost shouts the moral of the story: "Never fuck with La Virgen!"

Perhaps it is the tequila, perhaps my exhaustion, but thanks to Lucinda's aria, I have a strong feeling that for her children, La Virgen is never really far away. The white caucasian virgin of Bernadette would have never thought of sending a decaying corpse to a drunk to cure him of his alcoholism. La Lupe seems to use weapons that her Aztec children understand and respect.

Lucinda, thrilled to have such an audience and to find a new bottle of tequila on the bar, is away on another anecdote.

"And my cousin, you know my cousin?" Without expecting any answer, she soars on. "My cousin Antonio, he was a cab driver. He was really ugly—*really* ugly. And he wanted to get married. But the girls would run, ugly as he was. Then he went to see a *bruja,* who told him it would take years for him to find a wife, but that eventually he would, that Guadalupe would give him a good, loving wife. But Antonio—he is my father's godson—stubborn as my father, a real pig— he wanted a wife *now,* so he went to see another *bruja.* But *that* one was a *diablera*—a black witch—and she told him, 'You will get a nice, beautiful wife soon,' but that, for that beautiful wife, he needed to come back for nine days in a row. Of course, he came back for nine days! One night, while working in his cab, he received a call from a woman who wanted to go to church—a lady dressed in black—at midnight. They went on for hours without finding any church open. It was nighttime, good Catholics sleep then, they don't go to church. Or if they do, it's to blaspheme against the name of God."

Lucinda makes a sign of the cross, at the same time scratching her big breasts. "Then, after hours, without finding any church, he decided to drive the lady back home. And when he arrived, he saw the same house where he had picked her up, but now it was all ruined and covered with ivy. And then he turned, and the lady wasn't there any longer. He started screaming and woke up everybody in the street. They recognized the lady in black. The only problem was that she had been dead for fifteen years! She too had been a *diablera*. For weeks, she called him at the station every night; his colleagues heard her many times. Sometimes, he would see her on the side of the road, waving at him, always in black. Then, finally, Antonio—pighead!— went back to see his *bruja,* and she told him that the *diablera* was using dead people's spirits to torment the living ones and that the only thing to do was to go to La Villa and beg for protection and forgiveness from La Lupe. So he went to the basilica and kneeled and cried for hours. And the black lady never came back, *never*! If you ask the Virgin, the devil cannot do anything against you! Not a single thing!"

I would have never believed that Lucinda had so many stories of *brujas* and *diableras*! This last one is even more interesting, since the *diablera* seemed to be also a *mambo,* a voodoo adept (from *voudun,* meaning "spirit god"). A *mambo* uses spirits and summons them back to earth. Voodoo is encountered mostly in the West Indies, Brazil, and Haiti. As I am about to discover, *brujería* has borrowed a lot from many traditions.

It is time to go back to the hotel—more than time—but Lucinda wants to mix more Isabellas.

"But you know now," she is still talking, "young people, they don't care about such things. They mock them, they think science explains everything. Idiots! You know La Llorona? We call her 'The Weeping

Woman.' Well, La Llorona, she comes to warn you of big tragedies. You never see her, you just hear her crying 'Booooooh.' " Lucinda blows her cheeks out and produces a strange, strangled sound, like the howl of a baby wolf. "Immediately after people hear La Llorona, they have bad news. But if you want to avoid the bad news or if you want her to help you bear it, just leave some goodies—sugar or cookies—outside your door. She will be happy to see the food and will forget to cry! My friends from Coyoacán, they heard La Llorona and freaked out. At that very moment, the neighbors called. They heard La Llorona also. So my friends went to the neighbors and they all started to be frightened together. Well, when they came back, their house had been burglarized! The thieves had taken everything, even the toilet rolls and kitchen things! They took even the old wheelchair that my friend used for shopping in place of a cart!"

Back at the hotel, my head swimming with Lucinda's stories and Isabellas, I read again part of the excellent *Mexican Witchcraft,* written in the 1960s by Claudia and Bill Madsen, a married couple, both anthropologists:

The big boom in Mexican witchcraft began with the arrival of the Devil. He came to Mexico with the first Spanish priests. Satan was the target of the Spanish even though the Mexican pagans had never heard of him. They learned quickly; they had to. The padres encouraged witchcraft beliefs by stigmatizing as witchcraft what they disapproved of. The unbaptized become witches. All who practiced non-Christian rites were wizards. Witchcraft was the nearest approach to the

Catholic conception of sin that was made by the Indians, and the padres took advantage of it.

The Christian dichotomy between the forces of Good and Evil was completely foreign to Aztec religion. Mexicans saw both good and evil in every man and god. For example, Tezcatlipoca bestowed prosperity and prestige in his role as God of Providence. But as god of misery and patron of witches, he caused anguish, discord and evil. No god or man was perfect. The existence of evil was a part of life that had to be accepted.

How sane, I can't help reacting. It is becoming clearer and clearer that *brujería* is a direct descendant of Aztec medicine and "good" witchcraft, a holistic tradition that disguised itself or adapted in order to survive. The Aztec *curanderos* employed an army of gods around Tonantzin to help them with their healings. The *brujas* have simply replaced these ancient gods with the equivalent undergods of Catholicism: the saints. Around Guadalupe, there are several with distinct functions: Saint Martin of Porres, the first black man to be canonized; Saint Margaret; Saint Joseph (he was the husband of Guadalupe, after all); Saint Isabelle; and even Saint Thérèse of Lisieux, "the Little Flower," canonized in 1925; which proves that *brujería* is a movement that constantly enriches itself and doesn't simply rely on a tried battalion of old saints.

The Madsens continue:

Witchcraft charges were not limited to individuals whom the Mexicans identified as witches. The Spaniards also suspected

native curers of practicing witchcraft. Spanish priests classi-
fied Mexican curers as good or bad, depending upon their
healing techniques. Good curers were those who adopted
Spanish medical practices and called on Catholic saints for
help. Bad curers practiced Aztec medicine with the assistance
of pagan deities. The bad ones, of course, turned out to be
witches.

Friar Bernardino de Sahagún further defined the Spanish
distinction between a "good" native curer and a bad one:
"The good curer knows how to bleed, purge, set bones, soften
lumps by massage, give herb medicines, and cure the evil eye.
The bad curer uses false and superstitious techniques such as
sucking worms or pebbles out of the patient's body. He also
practices sorcery and has a pact with the Devil." According to
Sahagún, "Devil" means "ancient Aztec Deities," of course.


Closing the book, I remember one of the other stories that
Lucinda told me. She knew "very well" a village *curandero* who was
married to an "invisible woman" who lived in a cave. The invisible
woman could take the shape of any animal and could fly, of course.
Lucinda told me that as if it were the most normal thing in the world.

I look at my watch, suddenly feeling depressed and not knowing
why. It is way too early for a Cuba Libre, especially after all those
Isabellas. I go out onto the tiny balcony of our suite and look at the sun
coming down and turning the light tea of the smog into freshly
squeezed blood-orange juice, wondering what I am doing here.

On Sunday morning, I take Holy Communion. I don't usually go to Communion, but it is the only way to see the Tilma up close at that hour. Afterward, I let Andrew return to the hotel, and I take a separate cab to Doña Rosaria, with a note pad and a tape recorder in my bag. Before entering the green ladybug, Andrew asks me, "What will you come back as? An animal? A bat? A deer? A plant?" I try to smile.

Doña Rosaria's street is, if possible, even more deserted today than it was during the week. The tall shutters of each house are firmly shut, and I realize how Latin American capitals sometimes look like bits of Paris minus the jacarandas. Then I remember the three jacarandas on the Place Furstemberg, near Delacroix's workshop, and the small converted maids' flat where Andrew and I first lived together on the Rue de l'Université.

When I ring the bell, Doña Rosaria herself comes to open the door. She wears a brilliant green dress with large pink hibiscuses on it that suits her. She seems in a hurry. "Wait for me, or better yet, leave and come back later. I am having a birth. They called me, I am waiting for the car."

I have forgotten that Rosaria is also a midwife. I suddenly wonder if the car will be driven by a Don Rosario. What a strange woman she is! Doña Rosaria nearly threw me out a few days earlier. Now she asks me to stay in her empty apartment and wait for an indeterminate amount of time.

Rosaria goes on. "There are some cold drinks in the fridge; help yourself. If you want to eat too . . . If am not back at"—she looks at her watch—"at five, well, that's that. I won't come back, so leave and close the door, no need for a key. I myself have been locked outside many times," she adds without a smile.

Rosaria stands in the doorway staring at me, probably waiting for the sound of a horn to call her down. "There is a blond woman behind you," she says suddenly. I feel relieved. At last, some psychic bullshit, the kind of stupidity that the James Van Praaghs of this world sell to those in inconsolable pain. Who doesn't have a blond woman in his past, when you look as Caucasian as I? I wait for the predictions, wondering if the rich marriage will come before the long trip, or vice versa.

Rosaria is suddenly calm. Her hurry seems to have disappeared. She looks into the air above me, as if she is trying to read a road signal without glasses. The wrinkles between her eyebrows disappear and she seems relieved. "It went all so fast," she says. "Way too fast. It wasn't his time . . . He should have waited . . . Things always get better." She speaks unusually rapidly. "He is better now," she adds, slowing down. "He says that it took time, but he is better now. He is in the light at last."

I understand, but I want to hear it from her.

"Who?" I ask, trying to disguise the tremor in my voice.

My skepticism makes her smile. "Your brother, of course."

A deep chill runs down my body; then a horn sounds down in the calm street. "¡Arriba!" Rosaria barks back. Before going down the staircase, she turns to me. "He said you need not worry about the ashes. He said that it is fine, *no es problema.* Your brother even laughed."

Then she laughs too for the first time, a bright, high laugh, and disappears down the dark staircase.


I remain alone in the musty, empty apartment with its currant-red walls. The living room also is currant red, with the lower part of the wall painted maroon. Baby pictures in golden plastic frames are displayed on pieces of lace directly on the TV set. On the wall gleam two enormous framed pictures, at least thirty by forty inches, showing La Lupe and Saint Thérèse of Lisieux, my favorite Normandy girl, who here has become a sort of virginal Gloria Estefan with an unexpectedly sexy bosom and a cross dripping with phosphorescent roses.

The two open windows are an invitation to a well-deserved cigarette. My skepticism has been badly dented. Doña Rosaria cannot have known that I had a brother who committed suicide on the day I turned twenty.

After my brother's suicide, his body was cremated and the ashes given to me. I drove all over Europe for two years in my little navy blue Renault with my brother's ashes in the glove compartment in an antique *pot à tabac,* a tobacco container made of eighteenth-century Delft faience. I was so confused about where they should finally lie that I kept them for an absurdly long time, hoping that some kind of divine intervention would guide me. At last I made a decision: I chose for his resting place a beautiful nature preserve, the Zwinn, in the north of Belgium.

The entrance to the preserve was located on Dutch territory, so I needed to cross the border. The customs officers sniffed the little chips of bone for ages, certain to have found a new form of crack. After being at last set free, I arrived in a gigantic field of sand. It was covered with seagull nests, filled with enormous heaven-blue eggs. The place was forbidden to tourists. Each time I approached a nest too closely, a seagull screamed and lunged toward me, missing my face or legs by only inches. At the top of the highest dune, I finally stopped and decided that this was the right place. I grabbed a handful of what had been my brother. At that very moment, a heavy rain, vertical and mingled with sea water, fell like a death sentence. The first tablespoon of ashes looked more like plant food than the blue-gray cloud my Byronesque imagination was expecting. Disappointed, I packed back into the container a nearly complete brother and took the road back to Paris with him aboard once more, minus a handful. A year or so later, after a visit to my sister's country house, I walked back to my car and noticed the empty Delft pot on the floor. My niece, then three or four, was sitting on the granite staircase, conscientiously exterminating a colony of ants. I gestured to the empty pot, and with no need for further questions, she said, "Fish pond," and went on with her massacres.

Years later, in a small flat painted in currant red in a suburb of Mexico City, my dead brother came to tell me that it was okay that his ashes lay on the bottom of our sister's fish pond.

Rosaria comes back nearly immediately. "These kids, they don't know anything. They don't even know when the baby is coming. This kid won't arrive before five days." She paused. "No, seven days—the baby will arrive in a week exactly."

I want to ask her if it is her midwife experience or a psychic gift that brings her that certainty, but I don't. I also want to ask her more about my brother. But there also I don't dare. I decide to concentrate on a lighted red candle, a *votiva* of six days, easy to find in every U.S. supermarket, in the Mexican food section.

"Lucinda mentioned several times that red candles are essential. Why red?"

"Everybody always used red candles around me, so I do the same. It's for the power. Some say for good luck, but good luck and power are brothers, so it's the same."

"Why do you say that?"

"Many people come to me telling me they have problems, and they wonder why God is after them and why they are punished that way. I always tell them, 'Try to figure what God is telling you.' "

"So, in short; to call up the divine power, a red candle helps?"

"Yes. The divine power is always there if you ask with a pure heart, candle or no candle. But I've seen so many women in my family use red candles that it became something that I do too. I think it helps. If not, nobody would keep doing it forever. There is a special day for red candles, it's Candelaria [Candlemas, February 2]. That day, you light a candle for luck and prosperity for the year to come. It's also the day when the babies are blessed. It's the day of the purification of Nuestra Señora."

Rosaria stands up because the water in the teakettle is boiling; she comes back with Sanka instant coffee and sugar on a tray and pours it in two souvenir mugs from San Diego's SeaWorld.

"What do you want to do with all of this?" she asks.

I don't find immediately anything that will convince her, so I plunge my nose into the San Diego mug. Thank God she doesn't ask again. Finally I ask, "Do you talk often with dead people?"

"They talk to me," she says. "I just answer. Some people call up the dead, but it's not good. You should not disturb them. I wait till they decide to come. Spirits have missions to accomplish. God gives them missions to accomplish. So you cannot disturb them without a reason. If they come, it's because they have nothing else to do. If not, it's bad to call them up. *Diableras* call the spirits up no matter what they have to do, and they call up bad spirits who have nothing else to do than the dirty jobs of *diableras.* They are bored, so they are up for anything, and often, they were bad people when they were on earth. Now they are between two worlds—no more in our dimension, but not in God's light. Ugly place to be." Each time Rosaria says *"diablera,"* she imitates the gesture of spitting on the floor.

"Do you actually see these spirits?"

"Sometimes. Most of the time, I hear them. It depends, but yes, sometimes I see them."

"And how are they?"

She stares at me, confused, and repeats my question. "How are they?"

"Yes. How are dead people?"

"They are like you and me. The difference is that they come and go as they want, because they are dead."

I can tell I won't be told anymore about the subject today, so I start on *brujería.* At that moment, the telephone rings. She gets up, sighing. I can hear her arguing animatedly for two or three minutes before she returns.

"That was Lucinda. She wanted to know if you were on time."

Then she smiles, displaying again her row of gold-capped black teeth. "She mostly wanted to know what we were talking about, but I told her to get lost and mind her own damned business."

I begin again. "How exactly do you help people? How do you know what to do for them?"

"It all depends on what type of problems they have. Most people have really minor problems. I tell them that they can do the job themselves. It's true—many people never receive help because they never ask for it. For others, it's health problems or household problems or problems with their husbands. Or with *diableras*. Then I can ask Nuestra Señora for them. My only power is in prayer. I don't have any healing power in me. Nobody does. We are just channeling at some moment the divine power, the divine love of God. The divine power does the job, not us, never! We just ask, and sometimes we receive!"

"I notice that you seem to mix quite shamelessly God and Guadalupe. Are they the same for you?"

Her eyes turn darker and I feel that her toothy smile won't reappear for a while. She seems to be thinking deeply. "It's simple," she says at last. "It's really simple if you think about it. Guadalupe is the mother of Jesus. He is God the Son, so He received Her wisdom. So it's good to ask her!"

"Yes, but who is who, for you? Is Guadalupe above the masculine side of God, Jesus and God the Father?"

"She is a part of God. No one is above God."

"And is God a part of her?"

"Poooh . . . maybe . . . I don't know. You need to ask that of professors. I don't know, I am just a stupid woman," she says, obviously not meaning a word of it.

"You always ask Guadalupe, and her only?"

"It all depends. For crisis and big trouble, yes; in other cases, I ask the saints."

"Which saints?"

"Oh, many of them. San José, San Mateo, Santa Teresita, Allan Kardec—"

I jump. "Allan Kardec?"

"Yes, he is a Frenchman from the old days."

I know Allan Kardec. Born Hippolyte Rivail in Lyon in 1804, he was—and still is—considered the pope of spiritism. He claimed he could speak with the spirits in a France shaken by waves of anticlericalism (which did not prevent Empress Eugenie and her ladies-in-waiting from having Daniel Dunglas Home and Eusapia Palladino, two famous mediums, for tea). Allan Kardec wrote two books, *The Book of Spirits* and *The Book of Mediums,* which are still widely read by his followers and can be entertaining if you forget the pompous, lecturing tone of his prose. Kardec died in 1869 from a stroke caused by too much indulgence in gourmet French cuisine (like another prophet, Edgar Cayce, who for half a century tried to convince his disciples that salvation lay in red cabbage and spring water, and who died with high cholesterol caused by his fried-chicken-with-gravy diet. But that's another story).

What a surprise for me to hear about Allan Kardec, a rather well-known figure in France but not abroad, another proof that *brujería* is in a perpetual frenzy of evolution. How amazing to think that what started as an Aztec dynastic tradition is now borrowing and asking help from a French Carmelite saint and a self-proclaimed Druid, both from the late nineteenth century!

"So, you know about Allan Kardec?" asked Rosaria.

"Oh yes, I've visited his grave many times."

In fact, I had spent innumerable afternoons as a teenager in the Père Lachaise Cemetery in place of going to school. Père Lachaise is the necropolis where France lays its—and other nations'—glory to rest: Balzac, Colette, Sarah Bernhardt, Jim Morrison (the best place in Paris to buy Hawaiian pot is at his grave), Edith Piaf, Oscar Wilde, Yves Montand, Molière, Isadora Duncan, Maria Callas, Rossini, and many others sleep there in sometimes hilariously ornate splendor.

Allan Kardec's grave is a megalith, extremely Second Empire— Stonehenge by Viollet-Leduc—where pilgrims from all over Europe come to lay flowers and requests, touching his bronze head with carnations, handkerchiefs, and baby clothes. The grave of Proust, across the road, is slightly less frequented. The presence of Allan Kardec at Père Lachaise, in fact, has sent many of the children of local florists to college.

When I tell Rosaria that I have often visited Allan Kardec's grave, she joins her hands in a movement of admiration. Finally, I have something interesting in my past!

"You've seen Allan Kardec's grave?" she repeats enraptured. I want to return to the subject of *brujería* and so ask her abruptly, "The moon plays a major part in *brujería*?"

"Moon plays a major part in life. Without the moon, there is no tide, no seasons."

"And no periods?" I add clumsily.

Rosaria shrugs her shoulders with disgust. "One doesn't talk of that—and surely not to a man!"

Instantly she turns icy. I think that I might need to resurrect Allan Kardec soon to lure her back to good humor.

But Rosaria continues, "The moon can help anytime, in anything. She makes plants grow and hair grow back. So many people invite disaster because they start their projects at the wrong phase of the moon."

"And what is a good time, then?"

"It all depends on what you want to accomplish. The waxing moon is good for everything that's about birth or beginnings or rebeginnings."

"Guadalupe has her feet on the crescent moon."

"Yes, she blesses the moon, she blesses the world. She is surrounded by the sun's rays and has her feet on the moon. She governs everything."

"In the Wiccan tradition, the waxing moon is the center of many practices. It also symbolizes the path to money and prosperity."

"Yes, that is true, and there's something quite simple you can do. It's a small ritual that helps you get money. But be careful to use the money well, not for drink or drugs—Lupe won't answer. Remember too that when money comes, you need to circulate it. A man came to see me once and he asked me to help him, and then he won the lottery! But in the street, he met three poor men, and he declined three times to help them. Three times, just like Saint Peter with Our Lord! When he went back home, his wife told him that she had lost the lottery ticket!

"So here is the ritual Purísima for money; it's easy. You need to go to a chapel of La Purísima (in Mexico City, the young virgin with long hair in a white dress and blue shawl, the model for Murillo's Madonna). If there is no chapel, simply buy a statue of her and a white candle, the best candle you can find. A vanilla candle is good, or peppermint, but make it white. Then take a silver coin; it's important to use real silver. You put the coin near the statue the night of the new moon. You say one Ave Maria every day, and you add, 'My Lady, give me ease to give happiness to others, money to clothe the poor and money to feed the poor and myself.' And when it's full moon, your financial situation will change. As long as you are doing good in your life, the Virgin will answer."

I am tortured by a question that I won't ask because she would probably just throw me out the window: If it's that easy to get money, why is Mexico City one of the poorest cities in the world? A white candle, a silver coin, and there you are.

Rosaria is still talking: "The waxing moon is the best time to conceive a child. It's also very easy—you give a long white candle to La Purísima and you say, 'Our salvation is in the name of God, who created Heaven and earth. Save our humble'—here you say the name of the woman who wants a child—'who hopes only in you, O my Lord.' You repeat this every day until the full moon, and it's easy. You get pregnant!"

I judge by the number of pregnant women and crying babies in Mexico City that the prayer must really work.

Rosaria adds, "My mother had a prayer to choose the sex of your child, but the prayer died with her. I know a *curandera* that knows a trick. She brings a present to San Martín de Porres for her client to have a boy."

"What present?"

"To have a boy, you bring two hazelnuts in a red handkerchief and put them at the feet of San Martín. But I don't know the prayer."

Two hazelnuts. Even heaven must react fast to such an explicit symbol.

I offer to pause the tape recorder for a few minutes. In the beginning, Rosaria looked at it as if it were a cobra ready to strike. She gets
up and goes to the kitchen. A few minutes later, she comes back. She
puts on more lipstick. I ask if I may use her phone. She says, "No, it's
too late in the afternoon." I assure her that it is all right, that I just need
to call my hotel, it's a local call. She says no again. She tells me to go to
a public phone booth in the street. She even gives me some pesos for
it. What is the mystery of her telephone that she won't let me use it?

In the booth, I dial my number. On the phone itself are plastered
the following instructions: "Don't stay on too long, someone might
try to call *you*." (who?) "Keep this place as clean as you have found it."
And the best: "Calls are expensive. Be clear, concise, and to the point."
Mexico City has many of these colorful mysteries. Another is the one
we've baptized "credit card lottery." Some businesses accept our credit
card only if it has certain numbers. If it doesn't, they won't even try it,
no matter if it's Amex, Visa, whatever. The company doesn't matter. It's
the number you get when you add up all the digits that interests them.

After my call, when I reenter Rosaria's apartment, I find she has
prepared a small plate of dried fruits, grilled bananas, and nuts. Since
she shows me her kind side, I summon up the courage to ask her why
she wouldn't let me use her phone.

"What does it matter to you? You've placed your call, so what?"
she snaps back. Then she calms down. "There is only my husband and
my son here with me. The phone isn't used to other voices."

I decide to say nothing and turn the tape recorder back on.

"How do you become a *bruja*?" I ask in my most convincing re-
porter's voice.

"*Curandera*, please."

"How do you become a *curandera*?"

"You are born a *curandera*. My mother was a healer, my grand-mother was, my son will be. My father was an *adivino*. He used to deal with the sun. He didn't like the moon. He identified the sun with God the Father. My father was a Tepehua Indian. He used to call the earth Moctezuma."

"Like the emperor?"

"Yes, it was something that remained from the old country, from the time when people thought the emperor could do anything."

"How did you find out you were a *curandera*?"

"I am my mother's daughter, aren't I? Well, I was three years old and went to the dentist. I saw a trumpet, a flying trumpet. I was the only one to see it. What a beautiful trumpet it was, like an angel's. It would soar up and down like a fish, without any visible hand to move it. Afterward, I told my mother, and she said, 'I saw it too.' Later, we learned that the dentist's father had just died and that he liked his trumpet so much he had been buried with it."

"And was your mother surprised?"

"No, not surprised; why would have she been surprised? She saw the trumpet too! She just knew it was time for me to learn the prayers."

"So it's just a question of learning prayers? Anybody can become a *curandera*?"

She gives me an icy look, and for a moment I think she is going to take away the plate of dried fruits and grilled bananas. "There are things that everybody can do, and there are other things . . ."

"Other things?"

"Yes, things that nobody must know."

"Why?"

"Because these are terrible secrets, and if they were to fall into bad hands"—she crosses herself—"that would be really . . ." The horror of what might happen is so great that she can't finish her sentence.

"What would happen if you were childless? Would your secrets die with you? What happens if you die before it's time to transmit the secrets?"

"Well, my experience will die with me. And still . . . I am not sure, but the spirit world knows the secrets. They would transmit them again by dream, by vision. We *curanderas* are just the keepers of the secrets. The spirits own them."

"And if someone makes these secrets public?"

"Well then, she would become a *diablera*. She would lose her power. She would turn to the darkness."

"But as you said, there are secrets available to everybody?"

"Wait a minute! Don't believe that these prayers are like those magic books where all you have to do is plant three black beans during full moon and do a little dance around them, and *¡ole!*—all your wishes are granted. No, you need concentration and faith and purity of heart. Guadalupe can do anything. But she also sees everything. If you don't believe in her, she can't act through you, and if you wish anyone evil, she will send you back the evil upon yourself."

"Don't you sometimes yearn to pray to Tonantzin?"

She gasps, stands up and turns to Guadalupe as if to beg her not to plunge me immediately into the depths of hell.

"Tonantzin," she explains slowly at last, "is the pagan mother. The real mother is Nuestra Señora. She is *the only one.*" She adds this in a tone that accepts no concessions.

For a while, we say nothing. Then I clear my throat and begin again. "Do you need an altar to do the practices? Or do you need to go to church?"

"You need just a small altar. You don't even need a whole room, just the corner of a table is good. Use a stool or a low table, but keep it the same always. And you need flowers, lots of flowers. Fresh flowers are nice, but if it's winter or too expensive, a potted plant will do. Silk flowers are okay too. You need votive candles also, in various colors. None of these things is indispensable; only purity is. But that's the most difficult thing to get, right? It is good to have your own altar. My mother could work without one, but her altar was her heart." She crossed herself again and kissed her two joined thumbs with sad gratitude.

"Is your mother dead?"

"Yes, she passed away seven years ago. But she visits me often. She's the one who told me that I ran no risk talking with you."

Rosaria disappears into the little room where I first met her. She comes back with what I think at first is a family photo album of the six-ties, with a bright orange tapestry binding. I quickly realize it is *the* book. I haven't exactly imagined it covered with human skin, but I am disappointed. I wish it looked more Bible-like, bound in dark leather with strips of ancient blaten gold.

Rosaria begins rapidly, matter of factly. "Every request must be started with an Ave Maria dedicated to La Señora de Guadalupe. You say it in front of your altar or in the corner where you pray. Make it clear in your book that nothing will happen without a pure spirit. *Nothing*. It's better to pray in the morning before eating, but one can pray any time."

Rosaria then gives me in detail the following ten practices. If I were to respect the rules and legal procedures, I would label them "for

Doña Rosaria's Altar

entertainment only," but as she tells me again and again until the moment she walks me outside, "Guadalupe can do anything, *anything*. If you ask her, you are already saved."

The numerals indicate the order in which candles must be lit. Use a copper bowl or container for burning incense. Light the candles while saying the Ave Maria. Make sure they remain lit throughout your ritual; blow them out only after it is finished. And of course, never leave candles unattended. Make sure your altar is always decorated with fresh flowers.

Every ritual takes place in front of your altar, kneeling at the feet of your image of Guadalupe. If a statue is not available, a picture will do.

## To Rid a House of Dark Influences


Start by sprinkling holy water through all the rooms of the house; then walk through the rooms in the same order with burning incense.

Say the prayer:

> O Mother, most tender of mothers,
> The holy model for all mothers;
> O Son, flower king above every son,
> You who shape all things,
> Keep us, protect us, lead us,
> And be with us all the time, everywhere.

Then repeat three times:

> Our Lady of Guadalupe, I put my hope in you; and in the Father and Holy Spirit. Amen.

Repeat this ritual nine days in a row.

Mix a drop of essential oil of rose with a drop of essential oil of nutmeg and a drop of geranium essential oil. You can add cinnamon if you like (Rosaria says this is no longer done).

Rub this mixture on a yellow or gold candle while saying the Ave Maria and—the expression is Rosaria's—"while meditating on Guadalupe's generosity." The mixture you have just made is *aceite de la rosa sagrada de Tepeyac,* oil of the sacred rose of Tepeyac.

Light the candle and pray:

> *De la luna viene todo.*
> *De la luna aún el sol.*
> *O luna, quiero un rayo.*

> All things come from the moon.
> Even the sun comes from the moon.
> O moon, give me a sunbeam.
> Amen.

Repeat the ritual three times and let the candle burn away. According to Rosaria, it is best to begin this practice at the new moon.

## To Transform an Unfaithful Partner

Start by reciting:

> O Guadalupe, grant me my wish.
> Emmanuel, Sother, Radix, Jesse, Ely, Ela, Elohim,
> Tetragrammaton, come and help me, now and always.

Now, while he or she sleeps, tie around your partner's wrist a red ribbon soaked in olive oil mixed with mint oil.

Pray:

> O Guadalupe, Mother, grant me that [partner's name] will walk tamely along the straight and narrow path. May thou be blessed, my lovely lady.

The toughest thing about the ritual: You must tie the ribbon around the offender's wrist nine nights in a row and store it in the morning in a place known only to you. On the morning of the tenth day, the guilty one will be biblically faithful. During the nine days of the ritual, recite the Ave Maria repeatedly while kneeling at your altar.

## To Protect a Child from Danger and Disease

Kneeling in front of your altar, light a stick of rose incense. Then light the three votive candles and say:

> Our Lady, who loves children tenderly, have pity on us, have mercy on [child's name] on whom, in your name, I put my hands, and do protect him/her from hurt and torment. Evil, no matter who or what you are, in the name of the Virgin of Guadalupe, come out of this child. Amen.

Rosaria added: "If the child is present, it won't hurt to fumigate him and pour holy water on his forehead."

### To Find a Partner

Place pink votive candles in the candle holders. Put some fresh roses in the vases or use a rose potpourri. Then, with a piece of red or pink chalk, draw a circle around yourself. If you don't want to ruin your carpet, sit on a newspaper and draw the line around you. What is important is to be inside the circle. With incense and candle lit, pray:

*Madre pía, tu que estabas al pie de la cruz, la cruz de tu hijo, la cruz de tu amor, ayúdame.*

Compassionate mother, you who stood at the foot of the cross, the cross of your son, the cross of your love, help me.

Rosaria promises: "If you do this ritual at the new moon, you will be chased by dozens of beaux."

### To Protect Your Possessions from Thieves

Rosaria chuckled when she recited this for me. "You have no money for an alarm system? Doña Rosaria's spells will keep burglars at bay!"

Take two candles, one green and one black. Tie a copy of your house key or a picture of your house to the feet of the statue of Guadalupe. Light the candles and burn the incense. After three Ave Marias, pray:

> May Your Son, who was crucified between Dysmas and Gestas, protect our goods.

If you are afraid that your house might be burgled while you are away, leave the keys or symbols where they are; don't remove them after the ritual.

Doña Rosaria also advises: "If you want to, write out this prayer on a piece of paper and put it near your most precious possessions when you leave them."

## To Avoid Financial Difficulties or Bankruptcy

Light three candles, two green and one red (for power). Surround the image of Guadalupe with leaves or flowers.

Rosaria said, "It doesn't matter if it's only parsley, so long as it's green and grows."

Place a dollar underneath the image. Rub the green candles with the sacred oil of Tepeyac (made with essential oils of rose, nutmeg, and olive—regular rose oil does the trick) and pray:

> My lady of Tepeyac, in the name of all the saints, in the holy name of your Son, in the names of the souls of purgatory, help me get (back) [name what you've lost, or what you need]. Help me survive.

Afterward, say five Ave Marias and five Our Fathers. Repeat the ritual for nine days.

### For Protection While Traveling

Doña Rosaria says: "Do this a few days before leaving on your trip or do it to protect people you love before they go."

Take two white candles and a map showing your itinerary or a postcard of the place you are going to visit. Light the candles and say three Ave Marias. Then visualize Guadalupe embracing your car or plane and casting around you a golden light. Then pray:

Mother of Tepeyac, you whose children crossed the Red Sea barefoot, you who with a star showed the way to the shepherds, grant me a safe trip; and delegate your angels to guide my steps, so that I may arrive safely where I am going.

## A Ritual of Healing

Find a piece of rope long enough to tie around your waist like a belt. A red cord is ideal, but a regular natural rope is also good.

Now, tie it around your waist. While doing so, visualize all the negative energies, all the bitterness, all the bad feelings within you transferring from you to the rope.

Then, kneeling in front of your altar, pray:

Mother, if I suffer a violent pain, take it away from me; answer my devotion; remember me. Don't make me pay any longer. Forget my faults. I want to lose myself in your love. Use me as you wish.

Untie the rope and burn it outside the house. The ashes will be scattered in the wind. You can also throw the rope into running water—the sea, a river, or stream—but never into still water, where, Rosaria made clear, "your pain will be watered and will grow and come back and haunt you later."

Use red votive candles and sandalwood or pinewood incense. Place an object that is related to your suffering at the feet of Guadalupe. If it is caused by a divorce, put a wedding picture or a wedding ring there; if it's a death you are mourning, place there a picture of the deceased.

Begin your Aves. Visualize Guadalupe holding you. (Rosaria says, "It's okay to cry. You can even roll on the floor if you want to. Your mother won't mind.")

Then pray:

Mother, you suffered at the foot of the cross,
You gave him life twice—
In the stable, and at the cross.
I give you my pain, it is now useless,
I don't need it anymore,
I don't want it anymore.

(Here, see Guadalupe destroying the dark mass that symbolizes your pain.)

Repeat this ritual every day. Rosaria advises a brisk walk afterward, "to help the healing energies circulate like sweet fire."

When I return to the hotel at dusk, I listen to the tape I made. Rosaria's voice is low, nearly masculine; my batteries are old. While listening to her voice, I suddenly feel an urge to go back to the basilica and see the Tilma.

The cab drives slowly down the Paseo de la Reforma. Through the open window, an old, toothless woman with one veiled eye hands me a flyer for the "Club Select—the only place for totally nude in Mexico City." On the back of the flyer, Antonio Banderas flashes brand-new teeth for a Mexico-distilled Scotch.

This is the first time I have walked so late on the perimeter of La Villa. The tables of souvenirs have disappeared and so has the mantra, "*pesopesopeso.*" All that remains are two or three hard-nosed rosary sellers. Their candles have melted in the sun. An old man with a red bandanna sells me two for the price of one; he is quick to leave. When I look more closely I realize that the two candles I bought have no wicks.

In the last open pharmacy, I buy toothpaste. The plump woman behind the counter hands me the same old tract: *"Este hogar es católico. No aceptamos propaganda protestante ni de otras sectas"* (This place is Catholic—we don't accept Protestant propaganda or that of other sects). When she discovers the diamond in my left ear, she is repelled and assures me that men wearing earrings—we know what that means!—will burn in hell. But the cross around my neck cools her down. "I thought you were English and Protestant!" Suddenly, the eternal flames seem to grow dimmer. She points out to me a tray of small cut brownies on the counter.

"*¿Puedo probar?*" I ask. May I taste?

She smiles broadly with a grin composed exclusively of gold teeth, a sign of prosperity here.

"*Sí*"—Of course. In Mexico, one can taste and sample all the time; the national pastime is nibbling.

I walk back to the basilica with my Rembrandt toothpaste in my pocket. The only life there now are poor people or cripples sitting on the stairs, glued like shells on a rock. I cannot help thinking back to the spells of Rosaria. Where is the spell that makes legs grow back? Where is the one that cures the horrible skin diseases that mutilate so many faces here? Where are the magic words that give back the blind man his sight?

It's nighttime now. Only one door remains open. I need to walk through the sea of suffering bodies to go in. A woman is asleep under the gigantic porch, four little children snuggled fast against her. There are no tourists at this hour, so all these people are here not to beg, but for protection. To pray perhaps to Our Lady of the poor, Our Lady of the crippled, Our Lady of the pariahs. Stupidly, I remember a passage of Hugo's *Notre Dame de Paris,* where the hunchback screams, "*Asile, asile!*" (Sanctuary, sanctuary!), while closing behind him the immense creaking door of the cathedral. Yes, everyone here is clustered like puppies around their mother. The miserable communicate face to face at this hour with no witnesses and no folkloric pathos.

A priest is celebrating mass in front of a tiny audience. I walk directly down to the Tilma. The rolling-carpet walkways are turned off at night. You can look up at the Lupe as long as you want. The gigantic candelabra draw shadows on the Tilma.

Quite suddenly, and for the first time, after spending years studying the face of Guadalupe, I realize why she is so familiar and has always been. The first time I consciously saw the Tilma, it was at the Mission Dolores in San Francisco six years ago. I had bought some holy cards there. Among them, for no particular reason, was a portrait of "The empress of the Americas." Written on the back, I remember, were a few lines about the story of Juan Diego. But now I realize my familiarity with the Virgin of Guadalupe is far more ancient, like a piece of music that you recall again and again without ever knowing its title.

Guadalupe—Our Lady of Berzee. It is the same face. Of course, the two images represent the same woman, so it's all too logical. The same eyes, the same inclination of the face, the same grave sadness in the slightly lowered half-closed eyes. Our Lady of Berzee, the first image of the Virgin I ever saw.

Berzee is a village in the Belgian Ardennes, small and lost in unglamorous woods. There is nothing typical or cute there. All the houses look alike, it rains often, there are gray farm houses and a lot of white and maroon cows. The same little hamlet repeats itself endlessly in that part of the world. Sometimes, you find a ruined castle (most often the surviving walls of a seignorial barn). But there aren't even a few picturesque ruined walls in Berzee. There's only one grocery store and one cafe, blue with the smoke of the cigarettes of the old men that seem to spend their lives there, cracking dirty jokes when a woman appears. At the lowest angle of the village stands a stocky church with a gray granite roof shaped exactly like those of the houses in the village.

From the valley, the church and the houses look like a hen with her chicks. In the corridor of the small church, you can find a pamphlet first published in 1947 that is still in print—the first edition never got used up—which tells you a lot about how often the place is visited.

The image of Our Lady of Grace was found in the ruins of an old church in Rome, in 1609, by the venerable Dominic of Jesus-Mary, a Jesuit. He was as good a painter as he was a priest and tried zealously to restore the image. When he finished, the painting's face opened her eyes and started to talk. "I will grant all favors requested by those who will pray to this image." Then she closed her eyes and remained silent again. The venerable Dominic had the miraculous image placed on the altar of the Santa Maria della Scala Church in Rome, and many miracles were witnessed.

In 1631, the image left Rome for Munich. . . . [Here begins a litany of the places where the crazy history of Europe took the icon decade after decade.] It is known that after Munich, she was claimed by the Habsburgs and literally stolen to be displayed in Vienna . . . Then, a few years later, you find her in France . . . The French revolution and its iconoclasts destroy many relics (the crown of thorns kept in the Sainte-Chapelle in Paris will be burned in 1790). The miraculous image is lost till 1887, when it is found again in Soignies, Belgium, another of these 'small villages.' [What a divine fall, to go from Rome, Vienna, Paris, to Soignies. In American terms, you could substitute New York, Boston, Los Angeles, and Jericho, Vermont.] In 1909, the image was trans-

ferred to the church of Berzee. Just before World War II,
the image will warn a church full of pilgrims against the evil
of war.

Why did the Virgin choose such a humble, even forlorn place?
One day, I asked the parish priest. He told me, "Our Lady has something to do here. Just what, we don't know and it's not our business,
but she came here for a reason known only by her. It's the divine will.
Who would know Bethlehem if Christ hadn't been born there?" A
wise man . . .

Berzee was the first shrine of the Virgin I ever visited. I was eight
and it was the first time I had ever walked into a Catholic church. I
hadn't been raised a Catholic—my father was a Calvinist—and to be
among these gleaming gold-and-red velvets, flickering candles, and
stained-glass windows was, for me, like being at Universal Studios. As
I walked toward the altar—all those candles!—an ancient priest appeared out of the shadows suddenly and grabbed my arm violently,
telling me it was *forbidden* to walk there—*forbidden!* I backed up, thoroughly scared. Then I saw, to the left of the forbidden main altar, the
most adorable face, framed in gold and silver and surrounded by fading bouquets of flowers. I decided to go and sit nearby. Nobody seemed
to think it was "forbidden" to be there. I didn't pray. I think, if I remember correctly, that I tried to blow out the candles one by one.

For more than twenty years I have never gone back to Belgium
without visiting her. I don't always pray, but if I were to miss her, it
would be like neglecting an old parent. Each time I go back, the church
seems smaller than the time before. All the walls are covered with marble ex-votos with golden words expressing thanks for a marriage, a

successful surgery, an inheritance, a conversion. Some plaques bear far-away names like Tasmania or Honolulu. Nowadays, there is no more room left for marble ex-votos. They are painted on vellum and kept in a big, thick book, near the candleholder.

Our Lady of Guadalupe, Our Lady of Berzee; the same face. The only rational explanation would be that the venerable Dominic found inspiration in the Mexican image while repainting the icon. It is known and documented that as early as 1572, two or three copies of the Tilma were traveling around Europe, offered to the veneration of pilgrims. But why would I try to find a logical theory for an image miraculously printed by an unknown method on a cloth that usually decays after twenty years?

As I remember all of this, I lean against the gray marble walls to let a group of women pass. For a moment, their fresh chatter breaks the calm of the sanctuary. A young man carries his baby daughter on his shoulder. They both wear the same T-shirt with the face of Jack Nicholson in *As Good As It Gets,* here strangely rebaptized *Mission: Impossible!*

The little girl and her dad pick their noses at the same moment. The group disappears and I find myself again alone with the Tilma. I remember a story from the excellent book of Jeanette Rodriguez, *Faith and Empowerment Among Mexican-American Women—Our Lady of Guadalupe.* Rodriguez tells of her meeting with women at the basilica. She asked them why Guadalupe was so different from the other apparitions of the Virgin. "She remained," a woman calmly answered. "The Tilma is her daily physical presence here. She came in 1531 and has stayed ever since."

"She remained." How could it be said better?

I've visited most of the Marian pilgrimage sites all around the world. Each time I've tried to find a support, a secure foundation for my always-vacillating faith. I spent time in Lourdes in the summer of 1992. I went there by accident, initially to rescue my aunt who was trying to repair eighty-five years of wickedness in plush spas and was threatening to die of boredom, alone in a town in the Pyrenees. After I arrived, I discovered that, yes, one could die of boredom there, but also that Lourdes was only twenty miles away.

To try to describe Lourdes is a nearly impossible task. The only way is to imagine a mixture of the noise at a book fair, the smell of hospital ether and decaying bandages, and a fantastically organized camp market where you can find everything from the Madonna in every imaginable size to the greatest hits of Edith Piaf on the same shelf.

A big city has been built around the small village of Bernadette. The retailers are nasty and the lodging horribly expensive. To get to the grotto where Bernadette saw "the blue lady" is not easy. A park has been planted and there is nothing of the dryness and desolation you might picture from the old movie with Jennifer Jones. Everything is green, freshly mowed. The banks of the river have been covered over with concrete. Actually there are two rivers in Lourdes—the Gave, born from Pyrenean ice, and another long, meandering ribbon, parallel to the Gave, and formed by thousands of wheelchairs, gangrened legs, pain-twisted faces, purple limbs . . .

The wheelchairs have blue roofs that often are a mercy, for they hide many miseries. I've spent days pushing wheelchairs there from the entrance of the park to the grotto. Some were too moved by the place and vomited on me. Some told me their stories or stories they wanted to be theirs. I became a volunteer. Goodness had nothing to do with it. The only other choice was to play bridge in a local tearoom with my aunt. The small airport of Tarbes that serves the whole area is congested most of the year. It's possibly, along with Paris, one of the busiest airports in France, and still it has only two gates. It is nearly impossible to get a ticket unless you book weeks in advance. "It would take a miracle," said the Air France employee on the phone very seriously.

The only real miracle I witnessed in Lourdes is one that happens daily, and it's called fervor. The hope that arises from the mutilated bodies when they are in front of the granite cave is something beyond this world. I don't even think that they all hope for a dramatic miracle à la "I'm walking! I'm walking!" in the Hollylourdes tradition; no, I think that most of them feel stronger and supported there.

God knows grace needs to be strong in the vast swarming marketplace that the rock where Bernadette stood has become. The hole in the rock where the little girl saw "a young girl with a white dress and a blue ribbon around her waist . . . her head is covered by a white veil and she has a yellow rose on each foot" is now fenced by thick bars of metal that forbid access to all but a few grumpy priests. You pass them candles—also appallingly expensive—and they are stacked, waiting to be burned. The candleholders are always filled, so it's unlikely you will see your candle burning. Horrible stories of never-burned and resold candles circulate. The row of wheelchairs has time to say one quick Ave Maria—I checked the timing on many occasions—and then one of the nasty men of God barks, "Next."

The spirit of Bernadette, who ended her memoirs with "Her eyes were blue," is far away from these places. Corporate Catholicism strikes again! On the way to the Basilica of Lourdes, you can admire, encrusted in a wall, the mold that was used to bake the Pope's cake when he visited in 1980. Nowadays it is covered with a thick piece of bulletproof glass since some sacrilegious burglars tried to unseal it.

Still leaning against the wall, I stare at the Tilma. I try to become moved by it, but all emotion seems to have escaped me. I wish I could be teary. I try to tell myself sad stories about the death of my beloved dog and so on, but nothing works. I am envious of the ones there, the ones I would call unfortunate, who can raise hopeful eyes toward her. For a moment, I think of them as lucky, in the same way I used to consider lucky the waiters who worked on the Riviera because they got to see the Mediterranean all year long.

Our last day in Mexico City. We decide to make a short visit to the basilica. Our luggage will remain for a while in the cold and stately dining room of our hotel, guarded by the sad eyes of the ecclesiastical portraits. Before jumping into the cab, I check for the tenth time the piles of documents required from a legal alien with a strong accent to cross the American borders without any trouble. When we arrive at the basilica, we go and say hello to the el Greco-looking beggar. As always, a mass is going on, and as always, I am disturbed by the absence of any reference to the relic that's hanging behind the officiate.

I find myself remembering the pilgrimage Andrew and I made years ago in la Salette. Mary appeared there in 1846. La Salette is in the Alps, sixty miles from Grenoble. A village? No, a few peaks where nothing grows, too arid and isolated to develop a ski resort. Now there is a church and a convent-hotel and nothing else. All year long, the air is crisp and the taps give the world's best-tasting water. Once again the Virgin appeared to uneducated poor children, to two shepherds, a girl and a boy, and once again, she predicted imminent catastrophes and offered her unconditional help.

La Salette is far too remote to be a holy holiday spot like Lourdes. And the Lady of the Alps looks much the same as the one in Tepeyac: same large shoulders, same hips of a woman that gave birth in pain. There too, she took her flight in the dust of shiny rose petals, leaving the two scared children with this last request: "What I had just told you, go and repeat it to all my people." Once again, she left a spring that has since cured many immanent and transcendent sufferings. The pilgrim center looks like a barracks, and just as here in Tepeyac, the priest is king and the Lady—even though quite respected—is just the vague ambassador of her omnipotent Son.

It is the same thing in Fátima, in Portugal. The men of God there too, I remember, intone the same worn-out old formulas that dim her miracle. There, she came in 1917, a sad apparition in a sad country. There too, she announced the dangers of evil; there too, she appeared to three shepherds. On the last day, she ordered the sun to dance and it did, witnessed by hundreds of thousands of people. Two of the seers died nearly immediately. The last one became a Carmelite and is still alive, nearly a centenarian, in her convent in the Algarve. She seems to survive only to be blessed by every pope that visits the south of Europe and wants to see the living relic, and, considering her age, she has seen a lot of popes.

At Fátima, Mary confided three secrets to the seers. Two have been revealed; a third one was supposedly made public in April 2000 and related to the attempt on the life of John Paul II. But some say that the whole of it, which involves the Virgin's apocalyptic message describing Armageddon, was not revealed. Optimists consider the third secret of Fátima to be, simply, the announcement of the end of the Roman Catholic Church, which is also a news that would scare more than one pope—and justify his silence.

Standing in the back of the Basilica of Guadalupe, I fight with all these Marian memories while looking at our own reflection in the gold-and-silver frame that keeps Mary a prisoner of the Church. Tears come to my eyes. This time I don't even need to pretend. She tried everything—she keeps on doing so—and she remains an enigma, something divine, respected (sort of), but underestimated, or worse, misunderstood.

If the *Nican Mopohua,* that nuclear text, were being read and integrated as it really is—a Gospel according to Mary, a new book of the revelation—the beggars outside wouldn't be there, nor probably would the priests.

Father Tissa Balassuria has written in "Mary or Human Liberation": "Marian spirituality should inspire in the disciples of Christ the desire to change things. Marian spirituality should promote new interpersonal relationships in which everybody is respected for what she or he is. It should enlighten our vision of our bodies and help us to respect them as well as our sexual instincts and sexual differences; women should never be victims of any discrimination. Equality should be instilled among men and women in the world and in the heart of the Church . . . Churches should be freed of their sexual obsession, their obsession with the body's impurity—and stop practicing and encouraging ostracism and discrimination: To survive, the Church must recognize that it needs an urgent transformation and admit that God can talk to others through the intermediary of texts, guides, and forms of philosophy other than those of Rome."

For words like these and many others, Father Balassuria, dean of the Roman Church of Sri Lanka, was condemned to silence; then, on January 2, 1997, after four years of humiliation and being spied on, excommunicated for heresy. Like many others before him, from Jan Hus to Leonardo Boff, Father Balassuria was silenced for the crime of practicing the Gospels as they were written. Recently he was admitted back into the Catholic Church, but only because old and under extreme pressure, he recanted most of what he had written.

Looking at the Tilma, I suddenly realize that all of the different people I've spoken to in Mexico are right in their own way about Guadalupe. She is a gigantic mosaic. Yes, "she remained here" and has kept the country together. How much more she could do if she were listened to, in place of being blindly worshipped.

On the steps of the basilica, pirated tapes seduce the tourists. *Mañanitas* are mixed with American songs of the eighties. Two songs play at the same time, one exalting the glory of Tepeyac and comparing the Mother of God to a large crimson rose, and then, while the singer catches his breath, Duran Duran suddenly takes over.

I go down to the Tilma; I look at her and tell her I am going to miss her. The physical presence I've been hoping to experience for days, without any result, is now, quite suddenly, overwhelmingly intense. A group of French tourists arrives. The guide briefly refers to Juan Diego and what he calls "the legend." He finishes by telling his sheep that the next stop is the anthropological museum and that they must leave their cameras in the bus because photographs are forbidden there.

I run through the official souvenir shop. Outside, the light is blinding, white, radiant. How can such poverty exist in such a light? We want to walk on Tepeyac Hill once more, one last time. We see a sign: "Museo de la Basilica." It turns out to be an annex stuck at the back of the old crumbling basilica. We are the only ones to walk its long corridors where, hung much too close to one another, are displayed admirable *retablos* (sometimes painted on cigar boxes) left through the centuries by grateful souls, thanking her for making life more livable.

Like in a French vaudeville play, a tiny mustachioed man suddenly appears by a huge tapestry showing Guadalupe blessing tractors and cows. He is a guard, dressed in the gray shirt of the basilica's workers—coming to us and offering to let us visit the old basilica, closed to the public. It must be his way of making ends meet. Still, we see his invitation as an honor, a final blessing before we go on our journey. We disappear with him behind the tractor-blessing tapestry, like in a Vincent Price film where secret doors open in the middle of bookshelves.

The old basilica is undergoing restoration. The floor is covered with gravel and jagged pieces of concrete. It is obviously dangerous to be here. The hammering is constant and the air is blue with dust. Every religious artifact has been taken away; the walls have leprosy. A few pieces of gold and copper now and then testify to the past splendor of Mexican baroque. How many millions of people have prayed here over the centuries! The atmosphere of their intense devotions is unmistakable in a subtle thickening of the air, a gravity and lingering grief.

The little guard points his finger toward the large central wall; the structure of a big altar survives, red and gold like a forgotten pile of Christmas presents.

"There," he says. "There, La Señora, La Virgen...two centuries... there."

Andrew and I fall to our knees. The guard follows us, even though he keeps looking left and right to see if the construction workers are not laughing at him. What a strange epiphany to be here alone for our last time in Mexico City. So strange to end up where it all started.

I remember the words of Doña Rosaria: "When you go to say good-bye to Guadalupe, ask her something and you will get it."

I've spent days praying for friends dead and alive, for the world, for the forgotten ones, for a cure for AIDS, for forgiveness of my own mistakes. Here I am short of time. Despite the generous tip we gave him, the guard is beginning to show impatience. I'd like a cat; yes, a sweet cat. I always wanted a cat, but Andrew's life and mine have been so mobile and unsettled for years. And so, after so many grander prayers, I find myself whispering fervently, as my last request to the Queen of Heaven and Earth: "Please send me a cat to love."

A Mexican boy sits next to us in the plane that takes us back from Phoenix, where we land and go through customs, to Las Vegas. He laughs a lot and tells us the "good jokes" he and his friends—all illegal—have played through the years on the INS officers. If you believe him, they are just a bunch of idiotic power freaks, easy to mislead and cheat on, like old husbands in French farces.

The plane is preparing to land; the big boy is very excited to see the lights of the strip and leans all over me to get a glimpse of the MGM Grand Hotel. We find him again at baggage claim. He asks what we were doing in Mexico City. ("Why there, and not in Cancún?") He seems quite impressed with my answer. I can tell he feels some guilt at having been so open and relaxed with "two priests."

"She was my grandma's patron saint," he says. He grabs his suitcase with a big sigh. "She is quite a gal."

In June, we learn from the *L.A. Times*—that didn't seem to take it seriously—that a statue of Guadalupe wept in Las Vegas. One Saturday, we drive to north Las Vegas. The statue is in the backyard of a private home located on Dona Street, on the outskirts of the old town.

North Las Vegas is a desolate place of extreme poverty, its bungalows built to shelter the workmen of Hoover Dam, and the cottages put up in Bugsy Siegel's time are now falling apart: Many of them are fenced with rusty grilles as a gesture of protection from the potholed, gang-infested streets.

The small house that contains a makeshift shrine for the statue doesn't escape the funereal atmosphere of its landscape. Its owners took down their garage to make more room for pilgrims. Autobus seats are lined up, and the plastic statue, four feet tall in colored plastic, like the biggest model for sale at La Villa, is placed in a concrete niche. Hundreds of flowers, most of them plastic or silk, flood the floor around her. Rosaries, baby pictures, photos of smiling relatives and big and small dogs and cats are directly fastened to her with faded bits of tape that flap in the breeze. A group of votive candles of all kinds and shapes flickers constantly. We ask if we can pray, and two men sawing wood nearby look up and say together, "No problem."

While I try to pray, a huge, stinking golden retriever develops a fondness for me and butts me with his big head. When he sees that I am trying not to see him, he plunges his head in a bowl and chews noisily.

A man with a creased, sad face comes out of the house. He tells us he is the landlord of the place. A tiny young man around fifteen years old introduces himself as his nephew, but for Mexican people, as for Indians, you are always somebody's uncle after you pass thirty. The nephew wants to translate everything the old man says, even though the other one speaks fluent English. The statue started to cry one day. She has done it again since then, many times. The police came, NASA experts came, doctors came. They looked under the chapel—nothing.

They X-rayed the statue—nothing but plastic. Tears come and go. They've been analyzed. They are human tears; that is as far as science can go on this matter.

I ask the "uncle" if he has personally observed miracles. He scratches his two-day-old beard and says, "Well, there was that lady . . . She was pregnant and the doctors told her that the baby was dead. Well, she came and prayed, and she had a beautiful baby boy." He points at a pair of baby shoes that hangs from the grille of the chapel; then, smiling, he embraces the desolate street with his two open arms. "The shrine remains open all the time, all the time, and nothing bad ever happens here. Well, isn't that a miracle?"

He offers us drinks and invites us inside to watch a tape of the crying Madonna. We sit in a sagging brown-velvet sofa surrounded by plastic ivy. The tape is a succession of sequences, most of them blurry, sent in by the pilgrims who have come here and whose videocameras recorded the phenomena. Close-ups show tears running down Guadalupe's cheeks at different speeds. Sometimes an anonymous hand wipes them off. The nephew enters the room and breaks the silence.

"Many people came here and asked my uncle to do business with the tears. My uncle kicked them out."

The wife appears. She has red hair, seems worn out, and wears a T-shirt of the Mike Tyson ear-biting show at the MGM Arena. She brings us Cokes and smiles nicely; then she disappears again and a smell of fried oil invades the little room.

These people are poor. They accept this apparition, this strange privilege of their caste, with a devotion totally devoid of pride. They don't feel like chosen ones. When I ask why the Virgin should be appearing here of all places and in his backyard, the old man shrugs and says, "She decides; that's the way it is."

When we leave, the old man gives us warm hugs. So does the red-haired wife—even the nephew. He repeats. "Come back any time." He insists on the "any time."

Before shutting my door, I risk a last question. "Why is she crying?"

He looks at me, not really surprised, and says softly, "She cries for us."

It is now three years since my last visit to the Basilica of Guadalupe. I go there a lot in my dreams. I run in the empty basilica. I've had a recurring dream in which I shout to stop a mass going on, but this too disappeared slowly.

I've been thinking about the significance of grace and sacrament in daily life. In a wonderful essay, "Sacraments," the late Andre Dubus wrote:

> A sacrament is physical, and within it is God's love. As a sandwich is physical and nutritious and pleasurable, and within it is love, if someone makes it for you and gives it to you with love—even harried, or impatient, or tired love, but with love's direction and concern . . . then, God's love too is in the sandwich.
>
> A sacrament is an outward sign of God's love, they taught me when I was a boy, and in the Catholic Church, that there are seven. But no, I say, for the church is Catholic, the world is Catholic, and there are seven times seventy times sacraments; there are sacraments to infinity.

I have written this book mostly in the large white house where we live in Nevada; piles of books replace furniture and many rooms are guarded by—at least—one Guadalupe.

My writing table supports two images: one a postcard glued on wood, bought at the basilica, and the other a little plastic statue with a red-sequined dress.

Most people think that Las Vegas is a strange choice for us. When I come back from the desert at night, the city appears so fragile, like a shiny, small ribbon in the darkness rolled out against the silent immensity of the Sonoran Desert. The desert is all around us here and one day will take back what was stolen from it. Perhaps one day archeologists will dig the ruins of the Rio Hotel and think, "It was a bizarre kind of temple."

When a thunderstorm is beginning, the smell of sage haunts the air.

Three weeks after our last trip to Mexico City, a beautiful cat with the eyes of a sad child, "a cat to love," entered our lives. We called her Purrball. We adopted her from a local pound, and until she died in my arms on May 9, 2000, she filled our lives with the love of Guadalupe.

I am extraordinarily blessed to have Mitch Horowitz for an editor and for a friend. What a joy and honor it has been working with you. God bless you.

All my gratitude to Joel Fotinos, who bought this project years ago and waited for it patiently.

Thank you to Allison Sobel for her extraordinary work.

Thanks to Tom Grady, at the Thomas Grady Agency, for being the voice of wisdom.

Dr. Clarissa Pinkola-Estés, for being the red living flame of Guadalupe's truth; "Madrina," for all the insight, wisdom, love, inspiration, and comfort you endlessly give.

For Ariane Genevrois-Hanut, my sister—it took us time to know each other. Thanks for trusting the process and thanks for trying to convince the surviving members of our family that I wasn't *that* weird.

For Mollie K. Corcoran, the sister God gave me. Through tears, laughter, ups and downs, you've always been there and you will always be. I love you.

All my love and gratitude to Leila and Henry Luce III. You have been the most extraordinary friends/surrogate parents one could dream of. There are no words to express what I feel for the two of you.

Tender love to Gloria Vanderbilt for all your loving support and inspiration. Thank you for the beauty you give to the world.

For Sandra Lloyd-Smith: Joy to the World! That's what comes to my mind when I think of you. You are as generous as you are beautiful. It's a pity I cannot include your photo here. People would understand.

Love and admiration to Dorothy Walters, for years of love, friendship, and generous wisdom.

My undying love to Puli and Princey, my furry darlings, for letting me know when it's time to play.

More love to Nancy Steinbeck—"Good times and bad times, I've seen 'em all and, my dear, am still here." Nobody illustrates that song better than you. Thanks for all your love, humor, and enthusiasm.

Jan Phillips, Our Lady of Photography—You are the real thing. The rest of us are just taking pictures.

Deepest gratitude and love to Paul Todisco, who was always there for everything.

My gratitude to all the people who made my stays in Mexico City so rewarding.

May the Mother protect you all.

An award-winning author and photographer, Eryk Hanut (www.erykhanut.com) has created projects ranging from an admired memoir of his relationship with Marlene Dietrich, *I Wish You Love: Conversations with Marlene Dietrich,* to a celebrated pack of Rumi meditation cards. Photographs by him have been exhibited worldwide and appear on and within numerous magazines and books, including *Son of Man: The Mystical Path to Christ,* which *Publishers Weekly* named one of the best books of 1999, *Light upon Light,* and *The Perfume of the Desert.* Hanut has been awarded, with his spouse the mystical scholar Andrew Harvey, the Benjamin Franklin Award for best spiritual book *Mary's Vineyard.* Hanut, the director for the Center for the Divine Feminine in San Francisco, is currently working on his first novel and two photographic exhibitions. He lives in Las Vegas, Nevada.